Finding
the Right Counselor
for You

Edward J. Rydman, Ph.D.

Taylor Publishing Company
Dallas, Texas

Book designed by Deborah J. Jackson-Jones

Published by Taylor Publishing Company
1550 West Mockingbird Lane
Dallas, Texas 75235

Library of Congress Cataloging-in-Publication Data

Rydman, Edward J.
    Finding the right counselor for you / Edward Rydman.
        p.   cm.
    ISBN 0-87833-680-X : $9.95
    1. Psychotherapists—Evaluation. 2. Psychotherapy—Evaluation.
3. Consumer education.   I. Title.
    RC480.5.R95   1989
    616.89' 14—dc20   89-30439
                                                              CIP
Printed in the United States of America

10 9 8 7 6 5 4 3 2 1

To all of my clients who wanted or needed counseling —
who called and found the help that encouraged them
to work on their lives and
to reach higher levels of personal satisfaction and achievement

CONTENTS

9. The Stress of Counseling 109

Stress in therapy—The time involved in counseling—The self-examination therapy requires—Taking responsibility for yourself

10. Terminating the Therapy Process 121

When to end counseling—The termination process—The client's role in termination—Becoming friends with your counselor—Seeing your counselor for periodic "checkups" after termination—Checklist of key points to remember about counseling

Appendix 133

National organizations for local referrals

Acknowledgment

I want to acknowledge the valuable assistance of Bob Crook in the writing of this book. As a lay person in the field of counseling and a professional in the field of writing, he was able to help me put my ideas into clear and understandable language and to avoid the jargon that professional counselors tend to use.

Introduction

"Where can I find a counselor? Who can help me through this crisis? How can I go on? Life is not worth living any longer; somebody please help me! Where can I turn? Where can I find someone I can trust, someone who will listen, someone who will understand how I feel, someone who can help me learn what I need to do to feel whole and happy again?"

I have heard these and many more questions from individuals, couples, parents, and families who want or need counseling. During the years I was the national executive director of the American Association of Marriage Counselors (now known as the American Association for Marriage and Family Therapy), my office received many calls from people in all parts of the country, in fact, from many places in the world, asking where to find help. I came to realize that a need existed for a short, easy-to-use book that would deal with some of the concerns of those who want find a counselor but who are reluctant or even afraid to get started without first knowing a lot more about what to expect.

This book helps answer the questions raised by the thousands of people who at one time or another feel that their lives or personal relationships have lost meaning—people who want to improve their marriages or get divorced, parents who want to do a better job of raising their children, dealing with their teenagers, or making their own aging parents more comfortable, and people who may need a new direction, a new career, a new love, a different way of seeing the world, or a new sense of meaning to life.

You may be one of these people.

Many people are not sure of themselves, are uneasy about calling for help, or are afraid that others might think that they are weak, or sick, or weird, or stupid. They put off calling for help because they are afraid of what others might think of them—or sometimes even what the counselor might think of them.

Sometimes a person calling me would start out something like this: "I have a question to ask about counseling. I know that you might think this question is stupid—" Then he would stammer and hesitate as he tried to frame the question. My response to such a person was, and still is: "The only stupid question is the one you don't ask! Any and every question is worth asking!" In plain language, ask the counselor, referral person, or agency any and every question that you have or think about. No question is too dumb, impertinent, or personal to ask.

For example, there are times for almost all parents when they feel anger toward their children. Parents sometimes want to punish them for being "bad," for doing things that they shouldn't do or for failing to do things that their parents want them to do. How far should a parent go in spanking or striking his child with a ruler, hairbrush, strap, belt, or hand? When is physical punishment too much? When is it alright? When does punishment become child abuse? These are the kinds of questions many people are hesitant to ask a counselor. Yet these are good questions to discuss with a counselor if you find yourself in this situation. The frequency and intensity of child abuse has increased tremendously. Many more cases are never brought to the attention of authorities but occur in the privacy of the home. Calling a counselor to talk over the stresses and strains of parenting may be a deterrent to child abuse. It would show intelligence and strength, not stupidity or weakness, and it certainly wouldn't be sick or weird.

Others who want counseling may hold back out of a fear of counselors. They may be apprehensive about losing their power of choice or afraid that counselors have a special skill that gives them the power to control the lives of other people. Professional counselors are there to help you—not abuse you or use you for their own purposes. They have no magical power, no strength to make you do anything that you don't want to do. Some people are afraid they might be hypnotized into doing something against their wills. That is the stuff of which television shows and movies are made. It doesn't happen in real life. If something that a counselor does or suggests doesn't seem right—stop. Don't do it. Get out. Terminate your sessions. Remember, you set the limits of your behavior.

There have been some cases in which counselors have done a poor job—kept people coming for appointments when counseling was no longer necessary or even engaged in illegal, immoral, and unprofessional behavior with their clients or patients. But this happens with counselors no more than it does with doctors, lawyers, ministers, teachers, or others who work closely with people. There is no excuse for such behavior, but don't let yourself be trapped. You can recognize if and when such things begin. Report them to professional organizations or other authorities. There is no reason for you to be a victim. Be responsible for yourself.

There are helpers out there, good, professional counselors, who, by education, training, personal qualities, and experience have demonstrated their ability to work with those who are depressed, anxious, upset, angry, worried, or in some way or another feeling the need to make important changes in their lives.

In fact, there are so many helpers and so many different kinds of help available that it becomes difficult to select the counselor who is most likely to be helpful to you in your search for solutions to your unique problems. What is the difference between counseling and psychoanalysis? Should you see a psychiatrist, a psychologist, a social worker, a pastoral counselor, a hypnotist, a psychic, or a vocational or educational counselor? Do you need psychotherapy or marriage counseling? How much does counseling cost? Must you go to a hospital? These and many other questions are considered and answered in these pages.

This book also provides valuable information that will make more effective the time, money, and energy you will expend in working with a counselor. Achieving a good working relationship with that intimate stranger is a delicate and important process.

Counseling helps individuals, couples, and families to work through problems and find more reasonable alternatives and solutions, to discover their own strengths as well as those of others, and to learn new skills and techniques for avoiding similar problems in the future.

Counseling helps people live more comfortable, happy, and fulfilled lives. But the process requires work—work that includes examining, in depth, the important events and the significant people in your life. It means looking honestly at your mistakes and realistically at your hopes and dreams.

There is a general observation made by counselors of all kinds that women, more than men, tend to go to counselors for help. Does that mean that women have more troubles than men—that they are sicker or weaker or less able to handle their own problems? The answer is no. That simply isn't true. The conventional wisdom, the consensus among counselors, is that women more than men are willing to admit to themselves and to a counselor that they have a problem or problems. This means that they are more willing to seek rational and reasonable solutions to those problems. Men, on the other hand, have been raised or socialized to believe that they must keep their problems to themselves, to suffer in silence, to find their own answers, to be "macho." Perhaps this peculiar behavior is part of the reason that men have more heart attacks, high blood pressure, and other degenerative diseases. But there are changes lately in the right direction. There is a trend toward men becoming more open and more willing to enter into counseling relationships. And that is a good and healthy trend.

A principal emphasis of the book is to remind you, and all others seeking counseling, that *you are responsible for yourself.* The counselor is not a savior who does the work for you, who tells you what to do and how to do it. The counselor is a facilitator, a motivator, a co-discoverer, a catalyst who helps you to find that you have the strength to grow and to be able to face your problems and seek resolutions.

No matter what has happened to you or what is causing distress in your life, the way in which you choose to deal with it is your responsibility. Deciding to see a counselor when you feel that you need help in coping with some of your problems is the first step in accepting that responsibility.

How Do You Know When You Should Find a Counselor?

E at, damn you. Eat!" Anna shouts as she shoves a spoonful of food into Cheryl's mouth. The baby swings her hands wildly, knocking the bowl of cereal to the floor as she spits the food out of her mouth. She screams as she turns her head, stiffens her body, and fights her mother. Anna gets angrier and the baby only gets more determined. Anna tries to force some more food into the baby's mouth, but Cheryl spits it out again and screams louder.

This scene and others like it are repeated, over and over, as Anna struggles with feeding, diapering, bathing—the whole range of responsibilities she has with her baby. It has become painfully clear over the last few months that mothering and all the responsibilities that go with it are much more difficult and demanding than she had expected.

Anna had always imagined that having a baby would mean having a precious, beautiful little child that she could dress in cute little outfits and take to the mall in a darling little stroller. She had pictured herself walking from shop to shop, looking at baby things and showing her lovely little child to the clerks and other shoppers. Instead, motherhood has meant being stuck with a little brat who won't eat or sleep, who messes up her cute little clothes, and who cries at home and screams when taken to the mall. None of Anna's dreams about motherhood are coming true. A real baby seems so different from anything she had expected.

As for herself, she feels miserable. Her nights are filled with the baby crying and wanting to be fed, changed, and comforted. Tommy, her husband, doesn't seem at all interested in the baby. All he wants to do is work on

9

his Mustang with his sports car club when he isn't work-ing at his demanding sales job. The warm, tender feel-ings that she used to have for him have been replaced by a hostility that borders on loathing. If this is life, if this is marriage, if this is love—forget it!

Her doctor's response to her complaints about feeling miserable was to prescribe tranquilizers. She has been taking one before going to bed, another first thing in the morning, and yet another in the middle of the day when she tries to get the baby to take a nap, so she can sleep on the bed beside her. She realizes that this is not the answer, but at least she doesn't feel as wild and angry when she has the pills.

In spite of Cheryl's shrieking, Anna tries again to put some food into the baby's mouth. Cheryl resists vio-lently, again pushing the bowl of food off the tray, this time splashing the mess across Anna's blouse. Anna's response, almost as a reflex, is to slap Cheryl across the face. The baby is stunned at first and then shrieks in pain. Anna jumps up from her chair and runs from the room. She picks up the phone, dials Tommy's telephone number at work, and asks his boss to have Tommy call her as soon as possible. When Tommy calls, Anna shouts into the phone, "Get home right now and get this kid before I kill her!" Tommy arranges to leave work, calls his boss and explains that he has an emergency, and races home.

Anna was born nineteen years ago into a family with three daughters. She was the youngest. Her father was a factory worker, assembling mobile homes in their small city that was known as the trailer and motor home capital of the country. He worked hard as an assembler, making a reasonable living for his wife and three daughters. Mary Angela, his wife, was a good mother who devoted her life to raising her girls. She became an excellent seamstress, making all of her daughters' clothes and even establishing a reputation as a maker of dolls' clothes and girls' dresses for christenings and confirmations. She took pride in her ability and was proud of earning extra money with her sewing skills. Most of all, she took pride in the many compliments she received as the mother of such well-dressed little girls.

In high school each of the girls became a cheerleader and their mother made all of their cheerleading outfits. Anna, the youngest and the one who made the best grades, became head cheerleader and homecoming queen. She seemed to have a bright future ahead of her. Her boyfriend, Tommy, was one of the most popular boys in the school. He was handsome, he was a three-letter athlete, and he was in love with her. They were the most popular couple in the junior class and seemed to have everything going for them. And then, in November, Anna discovered that she was pregnant and that she would have a baby early in May.

They were devastated. After some stormy sessions with their families, they decided to get married right after the Christmas holidays. They decided that Anna would drop out of school for the second semester and that Tommy would complete the school year and then get a full-time job working at the trailer parts store. Her parents offered to let them live with them, since her two older sisters had moved out and there was plenty of room. They agreed to live with her parents until the baby was three months old and then get their own apartment.

Tommy was not making much money because the energy crisis had hurt the trailer business, and so they barely managed to scrape by. Their marriage and their young family was not off to a very good start.

You get the picture. Here is a lovely young woman with all the responsibilities of motherhood, with a husband who shares little of her life and who responds mainly to his own interests, and with a baby whose demands are incessant and who reacts to her mother's frustrations by becoming tense, uncomfortable, and unable to eat or sleep properly. Here is a young woman becoming dependent upon tranquilizers to help her face the day, a woman who is losing control, angrily striking out at her six-month-old child for acting like an infant. This woman needs help. This man needs help. And, in a way, the innocent child needs help.

They need a counselor—someone who will help them put their situation into a different perspective, someone who will help them deal with their individual frustrations, someone who will work with them in solving all the interpersonal problems that are fast eroding the dream they shared when they married.

There are hundreds of other cases, similar to this in intensity but different in details, that could serve as examples of the difficulties each one of us must face in living, loving, working, playing, relating, studying, and growing. Most of the time we are able to handle such problems adequately, but there are times when we feel overpowered or overwhelmed by them.

WHEN TO SEEK COUNSELING

When difficulties arise, when tensions grow, when depressed feelings take over and make you feel that life isn't worth living, or when anger or bad habits become so dominant that they seem to rule your life, then it is wise to find help. In fact, it is a sign of strength, of health, and of self-respect to seek professional help.

When relationships fall apart, when a marriage disintegrates, when a love affair fails, when a boss says that you are no longer needed on the job, when the company closes, when you must move on to a new location—these are the times when you should talk things over with a person who is trained to help.

Grieving and sadness over sickness or death in the family, the loss of a good friend, feelings of loss when children grow up and leave, finding that you must close up your old family homestead and arrange for the care of your aging parents—these, too, are times when seeking a counselor is the right thing to do.

Counseling is valuable not only when you are upset or distressed almost beyond your limits, but also when you are entering into relationships and situations where there are known problems and hazards that may be handled if anticipated. For example, pre-marital counseling is a kind of therapy that helps people avoid problems in the future.

Professional pre-marital counseling is valuable in helping those who want their marriages to be the fulfillment of their highest dreams. You can't eliminate the problems, but you can learn how to manage them. Counseling can help you do that.

Pre-marital counseling is definitely advisable for couples who are marrying for the second time, that is, those who have been married and divorced. This is especially true for those who have children from their first marriages. With about one half of all first marriages ending in divorce, about three fifths of all children have experienced family life in which there has been a divorce.

Adults have many adjustments to make with their new marital partners. Children have even more adjustments to make, usually without the same motivating factors that their parents will have. They haven't fallen in love with their new parent and his or her children, but they have to go along with the plans because their parents are marrying, like it or not. The children may not like it and that can lead to serious problems.

When either partner in a second marriage has children from the first marriage, the new marital partner has the difficult task of becoming a "mother" or "father" to children who have loyalties to their biological parent. This new "parent" will have different standards, rules, and ways of dealing with children. Loyalties to the absent parent may complicate issues such as discipline, affection, and love for the new parent.

When both of the partners have children from an earlier marriage, the problems are even greater. Counseling sessions with the two planning to marry, additional sessions with the children of each of them, and finally sessions with everyone together will help clarify ways of living and working together. Such sessions may also reduce or eliminate the problems that are an inevitable part of the joining of two families.

Here is a list of some other situations, problems, and events for which counseling may provide help:

anger	divorce
alcoholism	eating disorders
alcoholic parents	study problems
anxiety	illness
an affair	suicidal thoughts
abortion	pain
drug abuse	family planning
obesity	educational planning
job loss	career planning
serious injury	parenting problems
mid-life crisis	depression
phobias	adolescent adjustment
sexual problems	sexual abuse
child abuse	a broken relationship
desertion	death of a child

WHAT IS COUNSELING?

Counseling is a special kind of relationship that rarely exists except in the office of a counselor. Someone may ask if counseling is not similar to what a good friend would do. Sure it is but where would you find such a friend who would listen, consider all of the problems and alternatives, and then help you to find your own solution? Most friends have a tendency to say, "If I were in your place I would . . ." Your friend is not in your place and never will be. A counselor knows that and helps you to work out your own solutions, providing invaluable knowledge and experience in the process.

Being unfamiliar with counseling and counselors is no reason not to seek counseling when personal or relationship problems arise. When you are faced with overwhelming problems, the sooner you enter into counseling, the more likely it is that you will work through your problem or problems and find greater happiness and fulfillment.

Those who have gone to a counselor and have found help grow in self-esteem and self-confidence, have better feelings about themselves, and have enhanced interpersonal relations. In other words, finding and working with a counselor is a useful way of improving your mental and emotional health, as well as improving your relationships with others.

How do you know when you should see a counselor? Answer: Whenever situations seem overwhelming and too much to bear, whenever problems seem too confusing, or whenever you can't seem to find any answers, counseling can provide the perspective you need to see your situation in a different way and find some new solutions.

How to Find a Counselor

*M*ary Ann awakens and looks at the clock: 2:15 A.M. and Rick is not home. He had called from the airport in Chicago to tell her he was catching the evening flight and would be home by 10:30 P.M.

Now it's after 2 A.M. and he's still not home—and he hasn't called.

How can he do this to me, again? He promised not to lie anymore. Has the plane crashed, was there an accident driving home, was he mugged getting into his car at the parking lot? Mary Ann runs through all the same fears that she has gone through dozens of times before while waiting for Rick to come home.

Maybe he's had too much to drink and has been picked up by the police. She avoids thinking about the previous occasions when he became involved with a woman from the office and stopped to see her. Mary Ann doesn't like to think about that. Her tendency is to avoid things that are painful.

She picks up the yellow pages under the night stand and turns to the section under the listing MARRIAGE COUNSELORS and again reads the list of names. She has done this same thing dozens of times. Reading the names and thinking about making an appointment seems to reduce her anxiety. Once she had even called the office of a counselor. She only inquired about the cost of an appointment and had said that she would call back later. Just knowing that the counselor really answered and was available relieved her anxiety.

While she is looking through the list of names in the telephone directory, she hears Rick's car in the driveway. She replaces the directory, turns out the light, and pretends to be asleep. There will be no confrontation this night.

The next morning, when she tells Rick that she plans to call a counselor for an appointment, he explodes. He shouts that she had no reason for calling one of "those shrinks." He is perfectly capable of working out their problems. This is the way it works out almost every time. Choosing passivity rather than confrontation, Mary Ann does not call to set up an appointment to work on a relationship that is clearly deteriorating. Instead she lets the whole thing slide. She decides that she will do something about it at a later date.

This is an all too frequent occurrence for many. Making tentative moves to set up an appointment, then failing to follow through, and accepting promises that have been made and broken before, many people put off getting the help they need. And, instead of seeking a referral to a competent, known counselor, individuals take the easy way of looking up a name in the yellow pages without knowing anything about the person they are calling. That's *not* the best way of finding a qualified counselor. The telephone company does not screen the qualifications of those who advertise in the yellow pages. The telephone company has only one test: does the person who advertises pay the phone bill? Choosing a counselor by this means may be hazardous. There are better ways for Mary Ann to find a competent counselor and set up an appointment. And she could set up the appointment for herself alone, if her husband refuses to join her, and work on her marriage problems that way.

QUESTIONS TO ASK WHEN YOU WANT A COUNSELOR

There are some important questions to be asked by those who want help and who have reason to believe that a professionally trained person can provide that help. Where can I find a good counselor? Who can I trust? Who is really qualified to deal with my inner secrets, bad habits, sexual problems, fears, anxieties, overwhelming decisions, drug and/or alcohol problems, or problems with children, marriage, or love?

What would you like to know about this person to whom you will open your heart and mind and to whom you might expose your thoughts, belief systems, dreams and fantasies, hopes and ideals? You may want to ask about her training, academic degrees, and areas of specialization; where professional training was secured after graduate school; marital status, parental status, professional affiliations, licensing or certification status. Feel free to ask for such information when trying to find a counselor or at any other time in your working relationship. Counselors are asked these kinds of questions often and won't be surprised by them. A good counselor will want you to have all the information you need to feel comfortable with her.

WHO SHOULD YOU CALL?

There are professionals who are trained and educated and who have professional licenses, certification, or membership in qualifying organizations who can provide the kind of help that you need. These people go by different labels.

These labels can be confusing, so I'll explain a number of them here:

Psychologists	Psychiatrists
Counselors	Social workers
Marriage Counselors	Guidance Counselors
Psychotherapists	Family Therapists
Ministers, Priests, & Rabbis	

Psychologists—To use this label, the person should have a Ph.D. (Doctor of Philosophy) or a Psy.D. (Doctor of Psychology) from a university with an accredited graduate training program. A Psychologist with an M.A. or M.S. (Master of Arts or Master of Science) in psychology can do psychological counseling but only under the direct supervision of a licensed or certified psychologist according to the laws of the state in which he resides. He cannot have a private practice unless he has special permission granted by the licensing authorities for the profession.

Psychologists have spent years in graduate school studying various aspects of human behavior and learning theory, psychological testing, individual and group interaction, counseling and therapy, perception, and other related concepts. They must then pass state licensing examinations, demonstrating their knowledge in these fields. After that they must serve several years under intense supervision, demonstrating their skills in working with people in counseling and therapy before they are free to establish a private or group practice.

Psychiatrists—They are medical doctors who, after completing their general medical school training, enter into a period of supervised training, usually in a mental hospital setting, dealing with those individuals who are mentally ill and are hospitalized. They treat mental disorders with chemical and psychological methods. They work in mental hospitals, clinics, and private practice.

They differ from psychologists in that they may prescribe medications and may hospitalize patients. They are licensed to practice medicine, and they specialize in mental disorders.

Social Workers—These people study the amelioration and improvement of social conditions and social welfare and do case work or group work. They are certified, in most states, by certification laws which guarantee that they have taken appropriate courses related to case work, to counseling individuals, couples, and families, to group work and recreation, and to psychiatric social work. They also study standards of living and family and community welfare. They have degrees listed as Master of Science in Social Work (M.S.S.W.) or Masters in Social Work (M.S.W.) or Doctor of Social Work (D.S.W.), depending upon the university that they attended and the courses they took. They may also use the initials ACSW, which indicate their certification within their profession (Association of Certified Social Workers). They often work in social agencies, organizations, and associations as well as in private practice.

Guidance Counselors—They may use the general term "counselor." These men and women have education, training, and experience leading to an M.S. or M.A. (Master of Arts or Master of Science) in counseling and guidance in an accredited graduate training program. Some continue education and secure a Ph.D. or an Ed.D. (Doctor of Education). The educational program for people trained in counseling and guidance is similar to that of psychologists, but these counselors are usually trained to work in school or college counseling. Their training programs are often in a college of education. Many are now found in private practice. Many states are now requiring licensing or certification of such counselors, and the tests that they must pass are similar to those for psychologists.

Marriage Counselors or Family Therapists—Those who call themselves "marriage counselors" or "family therapists" are usually psychologists, counselors, psychiatrists, social workers, or professionals who specialize in working with relationships in marriage or family, or with couples who live together but are not married. Some universities have established training programs and are graduating people whose education is specifically in the field of marriage and family relationships. They will have an M.A., an M.S., or a Ph.D. This is a very important, emerging field of counseling, for there is much research and information available about marriage, divorce, childbirth and child rearing, spouse and child abuse, sexuality, mediation, extended families, homosexual relationships, etc., but many of these subjects are not included in the mainline professional training programs.

Because of the interdisciplinary nature of the marriage and family area, many states have chosen not to set up standards for counseling in these areas. Consequently, few states have licensing, and anyone who chooses may set himself or herself up as a marriage and family counselor or therapist without any training or professional background. For this reason, you should ask about the education and training of those who call themselves by such names.

Pastoral Counselors—These are ministers, priests, or rabbis who choose to counsel rather than preach, teach, and administer at their local churches or synagogues. Those who are qualified as "pastoral counselors" usually take additional work in the seminary or participate in other training programs to become skilled in counseling. Some clergy persons choose to emphasize counseling in their work with the members of their parishes or congregations even without additional training. The line between spiritual advisor and counselor is sometimes blurred. The academic degrees of pastoral counselors include: B.D. (Bachelor of Divinity) and Master of Divinity (M. Div.). The degree Doctor of Divinity (D.D.) is usually an honorary degree and not an indication of training in pastoral counseling.

Some clergypersons give up serving a local church and go into a private practice of pastoral counseling, but this is unusual. Most provide pastoral counseling to the members of their local congregations. There are radio and television counselors, but that is another matter altogether. Those "counselors" are often not professionally-trained counselors but are usually persons enlisted for this specialized religious service.

Psychotherapists—This is another general term that may be used by professionals, psychiatrists, psychologists, counselors, and others. It is applied to those who treat mental, emotional, or psychological disorders. There are few, if any, legal limitations to the use of the term. This means that anyone who chooses to do so may call himself a psychotherapist, whether or not he has had any training. There are crystal psychotherapists who lay certain crystals on a client's abdomen in order to promote healing. There are therapists who have a connection with previous lives or have a person from the spirit world who tells them what advice to give. Some are psychotherapists who base their therapy on the alignments of planets at certain times. All sorts of quackery exists under this label. Beware! Always ask about the professional background and training of the person who uses the label psychotherapist. Some are legitimate and some are not. Beware of psychics, fortune tellers, tarot card readers, palmists, phrenologists, and spiritualists. There are very good psychotherapists out there, but you should be aware of the different kinds of practitioners who use this label.

WHERE TO FIND A COUNSELOR

Once you have decided that you need a counselor or therapist, there are several sources of helpful information:

Friends and Relatives

A logical way to find information about counselors would be to ask among those who care for you, who know you best, and who have your best interests at heart . . . your mother or father, brother or sister, or friends. But how much do they really know about the counseling resources in the community? Unless they have seen a counselor or have had therapy, they probably don't know the names of counselors. They would probably ask their friends and others in whom they have confidence. This source is usually a reasonable one but, too often, is limited.

Many people are reluctant to tell their family members or close friends that they are having difficulty handling their problems and so are unwilling to ask those who are close to them for help in finding a counselor. Maybe that's the way you feel. If so, then you'll have to look to some other source.

Trusted Family Friends

You might call your family physician, minister, priest, teacher, or some other trusted person and ask for references. Some doctors, probably most of them, are acquainted with counselors. Because of their medical training, they are most likely to suggest a psychiatrist, a suggestion that may or may not be a useful reference. The minister, priest, or rabbi may suggest that you come in to see him, since many have training in pastoral counseling. That may be a good place to begin, unless you are uncomfortable about talking to someone you know about your personal problems.

Teachers, Leaders, Officers, Others

There are other knowledgeable individuals you may know who may be helpful—teachers, school counselors and advisors, lawyers, personnel directors, union stewards, etc. They may have done work in the community that acquainted them with professional counselors. Ask them for suggestions or referrals.

Occasionally, there are radio or television programs in which a counselor or therapist has had a part and has expressed herself in such a way as to lead you to believe that you would like to talk to her. The way that someone expresses herself in the media may lead you to feel that she is someone who could understand your problems.

Similarly, PTA programs, church lecture series, and other community programs sometimes have as speakers counselors who present their ideas and respond to questions in ways that indicate their ability to understand the kinds of problems you want to discuss. Interviews reported in newspapers and local magazines often present counselors in ways which help to prepare the way for self-referral. In other words, you yourself may telephone those individuals that you have heard or read about and tell them where you heard about them and that you would like to have an appointment with them. Even with these people that you may have seen on television, heard on the radio, or read about in the newspapers, you should inquire about their professional training for the delicate and personal kind of work involved in counseling.

The Yellow Pages of Telephone Directories

Many turn to the yellow pages, the telephone directory listing all kinds of services. With this source you must use extreme caution. Under the headings related to counseling, psychotherapy, marriage counseling, and similar titles, you will find listed together the qualified with the unqualified, the good with the bad, the professionals with the quacks. For example, under the listing MARRIAGE COUNSELORS, there may be listed persons or groups having no qualifications other than that of having a telephone. As I mentioned earlier, the reason for this is that the telephone companies list everyone who has a telephone, regardless of his qualifications. The telephone companies refuse to become professional screening services by asking about the qualifications of those who advertise in the directory. Anyone can be listed. You must use your discretion when using the yellow pages.

Many individuals may have letters after their names, such as Ph.D., M.A., M.S.W., M.D., D.D., or L.P.C. Some of the letters indicate academic degrees while others may be honorary or are for licensing or certification to assure the public that those listed in the phone book have demonstrated professional competence in the field of counseling according to state requirements.

One category in the yellow pages that may be helpful is the listing under professional organizations. The list includes members only. Such organizations include:

The American Association for Marriage and
    Family Therapy
The American Psychological Association
The American Psychiatric Association
The Association of Certified Social Workers
The American Personnel and Guidance Association
The American Association of Pastoral Counselors

In large metropolitan areas these organizations may have listings that assure you that those listed have all the desired requirements for education, training, and clinical experience under supervision.

Other Sources of Referrals

Other sources of referrals are the local Council of Social Agencies, the United Way, or whatever organization within your local community acts as a clearinghouse or assembly of social, health, and welfare services. There are some special services and organizations such as Alcoholics Anonymous, Family Services Associations, the Council of Churches, and other mental health associations that may be able to make referrals based upon working relationships with qualified professionals. They may not know all of the qualified counselors within your community, but they will know some and will probably make some suggestions.

This book includes an appendix of national organizations that can offer you referrals. A letter or phone call to one of these will bring you more information.

Help is always available. Qualified, competent professionals can be found in almost every community except some very small towns and rural areas. If you live in such an area, it will probably be necessary to travel to the nearest larger community. You may have to do some searching. Don't give up. Use the resources suggested and those appearing in the appendix of this book, and help will be found.

3

How to Choose a Counselor

M aria has just returned home from picking up little Mike after work. She hears Michael drive into the driveway. She holds up Mike and they watch from behind the curtain of the front window as Michael gets out of his pickup. He walks around the shiny truck, examining and touching each wheel lovingly. Maria has a sick feeling in the pit of her stomach as she sees that each wheel is new, bright, shiny chrome, and each new tire is one of those huge, oversized tires that he has been talking about. New wheels and big tires! That must have cost him a fortune, she thinks to herself. He has been talking about them, but she has tried to discourage him, saying that they would cost too much money. He argued that they would make the pickup much more valuable. But she could not follow his line of reasoning.

"Truck. Daddy truck," shouts two-year-old Mike with glee as he watches his father walk around the truck. He pushes away from his mother and runs to the door, trying to get out to see it more closely.

Maria feels dread, anger, and tenderness all mixed together as she watches her husband walk around the vehicle that had become such a barrier between them. He is so proud of that truck. He spends so much time working on it, cleaning and polishing it, and so much of their money buying new gadgets and parts for it, that she feels neglected and abandoned. Most of all it seems that Michael has lost his sense of values as he devotes so much of himself to that piece of machinery. Neither Mikey nor she herself mean nearly as much to him as his truck does.

On weekends, when the three of them climb into the cab and drive around, she feels his pride as friends wave and give signs of approval. And little Mike loves to ride in it.

33

But, more often than pride, she experiences a sinking feeling of dread when he reads those magazines carrying the articles and ads about more things that he could add to his truck—chromed lifters, springs, headers—and all so very expensive. That is the only thing that he reads anymore. That and the sports pages.

Maria works hard to earn her share of the income. She spent two years at the community college studying accounting and now she earns a good income working as an accountant in the state department of taxation. Her income sometimes exceeds Michael's because she is on an annual salary and his job in construction is irregular in the winter when rain, snow, and cold weather keep him from working every day. Sometimes he'll lose money by being off for days at a time. But he doesn't seem to mind, because then he can work on his truck.

It bothers her a great deal that in their marriage she is the one who has the responsibility for paying the bills, keeping the credit cards paid, and keeping their checking account balanced, while he is the one who overspends credit card limits and, on occasion, writes "hot" checks.

Michael's first words as he enters the house are, "Well, did you talk to the priest like you said you would?"

"Yes, I did, and he gave me the name of a counselor that he thinks we should go see. He knows the counselor and says he's the kind of person that you could talk to. When I told Father Garcia that you really didn't want to talk to anyone about our problems, he asked me what kind of problems we were having. I told him that they were mostly financial . . . but I also told him we were having some problems with our love life, especially when you get mad at me."

Michael becomes angry as he listens to Maria's explanation of the visit. "Why'd you have to bring that up? You know what I think about all this counseling bull. I can work out my own problems if you'd just keep off my back. I told my dad about your counseling idea, and he said that he never went to a counselor and he's been married for twenty-eight years. He said that you women are all alike. Always bitching about money and not having enough."

Maria expects this reaction. She is prepared and responds calmly, "Well, you said that you would be willing to go in, at least once, so I made an appointment with the counselor at the Consumer Credit Counseling Service. That's where this guy works, the one that Father Garcia knows. We're supposed to go tomorrow at five o'clock. If you come home right after you finish work, we can make it with no trouble."

Michael acts as though he's been trapped. He throws the newspaper to the floor, stomps out to the refrigerator, takes out a beer, pops it open angrily, and gulps it down. But eventually he calms down and agrees to go.

They meet with the counselor on the following day. Maria brings along the records for their Visa and MasterCard accounts and their checking account statements for the past six months. It's obvious that Michael has spent the most money on each card and that he has written several "hot" checks for parts at the auto supply stores. Those checks had to be covered by money Maria borrowed from her family. It all adds up to the fact that he spends a lot of money on his fancy pickup and very little on her old Ford Falcon or anything for the family.

Michael recognizes the counselor, Hank Hankins as soon as they met him. He's seen his picture in the high school "Hall of Fame"—he was captain of the basketball team when they won the state championship. To Michael's way of thinking, this gives the counselor a lot of credibility.

Mr. Hankins carefully goes over the information that Maria has brought in and identifies the charges and who has made them. He skillfully suggests the need for fiscal responsibility on Michael's part without making him look too bad. They worked out a plan whereby there will be no credit card for either of them until the cards are paid off, and Michael can write checks only after consulting with Maria about the bank balance. Maria continues to keep responsibility for paying bills and balancing the checking account.

Maria had carefully explained to the priest that Michael would not participate in counseling if he felt that the counselor was not a man's man. The priest made a good referral, recognizing Michael's attitude toward counseling and finding a person who would be acceptable to and even admired by him. They both recognized that finding the right counselor is often a difficult and delicate matter, especially if there is a reluctance on the part of one of the partners to engage in counseling.

The counselor expresses enough knowledge and interest in Michael's hobby and in his pickup that Michael is willing to accept the responsibility for his reckless financial behavior and to find ways of accepting Maria's skill in handling the money in their marriage. They even work out an arrangement that gives him freedom to buy things for his pickup—but only if he'll save up the money before he buys them.

WHAT KIND OF COUNSELOR IS RIGHT FOR YOU?

For Maria, choosing a counselor was relatively easy. The counselor was recommended highly by a person that she could depend on, someone who could be trusted to make a good referral: her family priest. He made a referral based on his professional understanding of her, of Michael, and of their particular problems.

Many people looking for a counselor are not so fortunate. They are on their own, or feel that they are on their own, in selecting one. There is no easy formula to follow. But there are resources available, and using trusted friends, family members, doctors, teachers, clergy, and local counseling agencies can help you find the right counselor for you.

Since there are so many different kinds of counselors, so many different schools of thought, and so many different techniques, the best way of finding the right one for yourself is to obtain a referral from a trusted source, someone who knows you and the counselor he or she is suggesting to you.

Also, since there are so many different methods or techniques for counseling, it is probably unwise for you to decide on a technique or kind of counseling and then try to find one who practices that method. Some of the many currently available kinds of counseling or therapy are listed on the next page.

Gestalt Therapy	Transactional Analysis (TA)
Rational Emotive Therapy	Hypnotherapy
Psychodrama	Psychoanalysis
Sex Therapy	Jungian Therapy
Reality Therapy	Adlerian Therapy
Bioenergetics	Psycholinguistics
Neurolinguistic Programming	Divorce Counseling
Cognitive Therapy	Primal Scream Therapy
Marriage and Family Therapy	Behaviorial Therapy

More important to you than the label or kind of counseling or therapy is the personality and training of the counselor. Is she the kind of person with whom you can work on the very personal problems or feelings you want to resolve? That's what counts, not the name or theoretical framework of the counseling. Many counselors are trained in and use a variety of techniques, according to the person and the problems presented.

FIND A COMFORTABLE WORKING RELATIONSHIP

You may find that the person you go to see is just the kind of person you can work with, and that's fine. If you find that he is not that kind of person, or that you cannot talk to him, or that there appears to be a personality conflict, there are a couple of things you can do. First, you don't have to make any more appointments—stop, right there. Or, you can have a few more sessions and work through the initial resistance before you decide. If you continue to feel uncomfortable about the working relationship, you may terminate and continue to search for a different counselor.

A comfortable working relationship between the client/patient and the counselor/therapist is probably the most important factor in successful counseling. This is called "rapport." Without rapport—a good relationship of mutual respect and accord—progress in counseling is much more difficult.

In choosing your counselor, remember that most research in counseling and therapy demonstrates that the kind of therapy practiced by the counselor is far less important than his or her personality and skill. Also, the professional background of the counselor—whether she is a psychiatrist, psychologist, or social worker—is secondary to her personality and skill. That is why having a few sessions in which you can really get acquainted is an important part of making the right choice.

PERSONAL AND RELIGIOUS VALUES AND COUNSELING

Your personal value system is very important in the selection of a counselor. Do nothing in the process of making a choice of a counselor, or in the process of counseling or therapy, that will violate your personal values.

For many people, the primary source of their values and beliefs is their religious faith. If this is important to you, you may want to find a counselor who has similar religious affiliations. The simplest way to find one is to ask your minister, priest, or rabbi for a suggestion. If you are not comfortable with this course of action, you can call the local council of churches and ask for a referral. Another source for a referral is the American Association of Pastoral Counselors (AAPC). (See the Appendix at the back of the book for its address and phone number.) Call or write to that organization for a referral in your geographical area.

Most ministers, priests, and rabbis must take a course or two in pastoral counseling, but that does not make them professional counselors. They may perform valuable personal and religious services, but that is not a substitute for a professionally trained counselor. It is possible that your own minister, priest, or rabbi is a member of and certified by the AAPC. If so, he is qualified by training, supervision, and experience to function as an independent counselor. He will let you know and will display a certificate acknowledging his status.

Television preachers often urge people to telephone toll-free numbers or local numbers to talk to a "counselor" who will answer questions. Those who serve as "counselors" by telephone are usually volunteers and are not qualified as professional counselors.

No professional counselor will try to get you to change or modify your religious beliefs. If you want to examine your beliefs with the counselor, you are, of course, free to do so.

In order to make the most of your experience in counseling, question your counselor, question yourself, examine your value system and your behavior. Do so with the goal in mind of feeling better about yourself, your relationships, and the way you are living your life.

If, after all of the questioning and all of the work with the counselor, you are not comfortable with the outcome, perhaps that counselor is not the right one for you and you may want to find a different one. That's alright. A different counselor will have a different way of relating to you and may help you to see yourself more clearly, and that is one of your primary goals.

Questioning and changing and growing are all part of the process of personal development and growth that should go on as long as you live. Selecting a counselor who can help you examine your life, clarify your feelings, and discover options and alternatives for living your life to the fullest can be an exciting and vital experience.

4

What Kind of Counseling Is Best For You?

D r. Dunlap reviews the notes he made when Jill telephoned to make her first appointment. She had explained that she was in need of an appointment at the earliest possible time. She said that she had her own business and that it was necessary to spend considerable time out of town. She was a "trainer" who met with large companies to train employees to work with customers, clients, and each other for the good of the company and employee interpersonal relations—in order to reduce conflict and encourage good communications. Her week was free and, if possible, she would like to come in during the week. Dr. Dunlap was able to see her the next day because he had a cancellation.

When he asked if she had been referred by someone, her response was, "No, I heard you speak at the Young Adult Singles' group at our church. You finished a series of meetings yesterday. I liked what you had to say and decided that I really should come to see you as soon as possible. I feel a little uncomfortable about calling, but I'm having a personal crisis. I guess I'm a self-referral."

When Dr. Dunlap greets her at her first appointment she shakes hands with a firm grip and a direct gaze and gives the appearance of a woman who knows where she is going and what she wants. She is tall, with red-blond hair, and she is very well dressed in a feminine business suit with a beautiful leather briefcase and a Gucci purse, all of the indications of a successful businesswoman. He recognizes her from the young adult class that he had addressed at the Methodist Church. She is the kind of woman who stands out in a group.

She takes the initiative as she sits down, saying that she enjoyed his series on human development and the stages that adults experience when they go through a divorce and move out into the world as singles again. She says, "That's why I decided I'd like to set up some appointments with you. I went through a devastating divorce two and a half years ago and I've recently started a relationship with a man I met in the church group. And that's what I want to work on." Up to this point she has seemed very much in control but, as she mentions the divorce and the new relationship, tears begin to well up in her eyes. She reaches for the box of tissues on the table beside the chair.

"Damn!" she says. "I didn't want to start out crying. But I'm really confused. My divorce really was upsetting and I want to talk about that later. Right now I've got to decide what I'm going to do about Charles and his children." She explains that she met Charles, her new friend, in the class for singles. He is a couple of years older, a widower with two children, a really nice guy. "His wife died about three years ago and he's been raising those children, keeping house, and working his job—all of them successfully. As I said, we met in that class and sort of were drawn to each other. We had a few dates and I really liked him—and the children.

"As we became better acquainted, he invited me over to his house because it was difficult for him to go out and to be responsible for the children. I really liked them. I felt so comfortable with him and the kids. But as time has gone on, I find that we can never go out without them. We can't go out to dinner without taking them. Then we go where they want to go, McDonald's and Burger King and places like that. Weekends we spend at his house and the entertainment is movies on the VCR—children's movies." As she explains the situation and its limitations, she cries. "We can't even have sex, since he's uncomfortable about having sexual relations in his house because of the kids and because he thinks of his wife. And we can't go over to my apartment because he doesn't want to leave the kids. I'm really frustrated!"

After further discussion, Dr. Dunlap asks if she would be willing to bring Charles in with her to examine the relationship and to find out how he feels about it. After some consideration, she agrees she'll talk to him and find out if he's willing to come in, and then find a mutually agreeable time.

The important thing to recognize, at this point, is that Jill made a self-referral. In her independent and competent way, she attended a series of meetings to hear a counselor speak to a church group. She found that he expressed himself clearly and she learned something about the way he thought, his philosophy, and his background. Then she called for an appointment. She recognized that, although she was a competent consultant, successful in conducting workshops for groups of employers and employees in work settings, she was not doing well in the face-to-face interactions of her own personal relationship. She reached out for help after carefully checking out the counselor.

But what kind of counseling would be best for Jill in her particular situation? She has the problem—she is upset about the way her relationship with Charles is developing. Yet the problem also involves him, so is marriage counseling the right choice? And the children are obviously part of the problem; he can't seem to leave them alone to spend some time with Jill as a couple, and she is beginning to feel deep resentment toward the children because of this. So would family counseling be the best alternative?

THE RIGHT KIND OF COUNSELING
FOR YOU

Another step in selecting a counselor is deciding whether you need or want individual counseling. Do the problems you face have to do with you alone, or do they involve you in relation to others—wife, husband, children, parents, brother, sister, friend, lover, partner, employer, employees, or colleagues? How you answer this question influences your choice. If you don't have a preference, follow the lead of the counselor, as Jill did when Dr. Dunlap asked her to bring Charles in with her.

Counselors know how they like to work in the context of relationships. Some do both. Which is best for you may seem to be an unanswerable question, but each of the different kinds of counseling and therapy has value. Let's look at some of the different kinds of counseling and how they work.

INDIVIDUAL COUNSELING

Individual counseling is where it all began—one person consulting another about some problems in his or her life. Long ago individuals in need went to see relatives or priests, physicians, shamans, witch doctors, and others who gave answers.

Now it is different. Individuals with problems go to see those who are professionally trained to work in the fields of mental health, psychotherapy, and counseling. The problems are unique and individual. The counselors that they go to see are specifically trained to counsel according to standards that are established by the counseling professions. Most do individual counseling. When considering questions about educational or career choices or job changes, or when facing fears and anxieties about one's sexuality, personal habits, self-esteem, or addictions, most people go alone to see a counselor. Individual counseling, one-to-one, tends to be the most widely used form of counseling.

CONJOINT COUNSELING AND THERAPY

During the last thirty to forty years in psychology, psychiatry, and psychotherapy, there has been a change going on. At first, almost all counseling or therapy was done on an individual basis, one-to-one, with the counselor and patient.

A transition has been taking place, and couple counseling—marriage counseling or relationship counseling—has emerged, based on the recognition that individuals live in important relationships that greatly influence their lives and their development. The next step was the recognition that the entire family, mother, father, brothers, sisters, grandparents, relatives, and friends, are all important in the life and development of the individual.

Why not, counselors asked themselves, work with the whole family network, the family system, or the marriage partners together rather than just the individual alone?

Conjoint is the term for counseling wherein two people have appointments with a counselor together and at the same time. They may, from time to time, go alone, but the primary work is done together. Such counseling usually focuses on the way the two people deal with each other or work on problems that affect their relationship. Such counseling may include pre-marital counseling, marriage counseling, couple therapy, divorce counseling, parent-child counseling, or sex therapy. Central to this counseling are the questions, problems, and situations that arise as two or more people relate to each other.

MARRIAGE COUNSELING

Marriage counseling is probably the most widely known of the conjoint therapies. It is a way in which the two partners may carefully examine the issues that are causing difficulties in the relationship or are dividing them. Living together in the intimate state of marriage seems to be very difficult for many, many people. In the United States today, approximately half of those who marry will, at some later date, divorce. If half of those who marry divorce, there must be, in addition, a large number of people who marry, have marital problems, and choose to remain married. In both situations counseling is very helpful.

Marriage counseling will help couples to re-examine their relationship, the reasons for which they married, the reasons for their present difficulties, and the emotional, familial, parental, and affectional ties that they have forged with each other and with the children born to them. They may find that they can modify their thinking and feelings, resolve their problems and differences, and not only remain married but recreate a relationship and an intimacy that may fulfill their fondest dreams.

For some couples, it is clear that when one or the other definitely wants out of the relationship, the marriage is in deep trouble and probably will not survive. For those couples marriage counseling may help to dissolve their relationship with the least possible amount of emotional damage to them and their children.

Many marriage counselors provide counseling for couples who are not in trouble, who are not struggling with ideas of separation or divorce. The goal of this counseling is to assist such couples in achieving higher levels of joy and satisfaction within their marriage relationship. Marital enrichment is a term used for this kind of counseling. There are skills that may be learned that enhance communication and the expression of love and affection and that improve the ways in which couples deal with their children, their in-laws, their friends, and each other.

PRE-MARITAL COUNSELING

The American way of choosing a mate is based on the belief that sexual attraction will be a sufficient foundation for a happy and enduring marital relationship. Judging from the number of divorces, that belief does not seem to be true.

Pre-marital counseling is primarily for those who are planning to marry and want to have the best possible marriage relationship. Before marrying, they want to consider the kind of relationship that they have in their courtship and what they have learned about themselves and each other, in order to make the most of the marriage that they are planning. Each of us brings into our relationships the influences, ideas, prejudices, and feelings we have learned from our parents and other relatives. The more we know about how they affect our relationships, the greater the prospect of a successful marriage.

Couples who are entering marriage for the second time should, by all means, consider pre-marital counseling. When a first marriage ends in divorce or with the death of a spouse, there is a considerable amount of emotional baggage from the first marriage that is carried into the second. Pre-marital counseling will be of considerable value in examining the past in order to make the most of the new marriage.

Many counselors believe that if more people chose pre-marital counseling, the number of people who are unhappily married might be reduced, but even so, pre-marital counseling is not very widespread. Most clergymen require some pre-marital counseling sessions before they will perform a wedding ceremony, but often this is only a token of what might be possible if more couples were interested in making use of the best marital-counseling techniques.

Organized courses in marriage and family living would certainly provide more reasonable bases for sound marriages but, as a society, we seem to be fearful of providing such courses. Courses in marriage and family living should be required in every high school. They would include much information that young people want to know about but which is not now readily available. Not only would such courses deal with sex, love, and parenting but also would cover how to handle money, borrow money, use credit, and many other important topics.

Despite the claims about the importance of home and family, few schools provide adequate courses on these subjects. Marriage and family counselors and educators try to provide such courses in churches, PTAs, and other community organizations on an informal basis.

FAMILY THERAPY OR COUNSELING

If you have ever been part of a family in which one member suffers from alcoholism, bulimia, drug use, delinquency, job loss, schizophrenia, or child or spouse abuse, you know that you and other members of the family cannot help being caught up in the problems. And you know that resolving such problems depends on the work of most, if not all, of the members of the family.

Family therapy is becoming the most widely used of all the therapies. That is because both counselors and clients are recognizing more and more that a problem affecting one member of the family affects the whole family.

In family counseling, all members of the family come together and work with the counselor at the same time. For example, there may be mother and father and brothers and sisters of all ages. Most of them participate in all of the counseling sessions, although there may be some flexibility wherein only part of the group may attend some of the appointments.

NETWORK THERAPY

Network therapy is a variation of family therapy in which others, in addition to the primary family, may join in the therapy sessions. This may include grandparents, aunts and uncles, or cousins. Sometimes the network therapy may include outsiders such as friends, neighbors, employers, clergy, and any other significant persons.

None of us lives in a vacuum. We are all deeply involved with others, and network therapy takes this into account in a useful way.

GROUP THERAPY

Sometimes counselors recommend group counseling or therapy. In this kind of counseling, instead of working alone with the counselor, you meet with the counselor in a group of six or eight other people. Usually they are individuals who are struggling with problems similar to yours. The group will usually meet for at least a ninety-minute session, once per week.

Most of the time the counselor will work with the entire group as a unit. Sometimes she will focus on one member of the group while the others are participant observers who will react to what they observe.

Group therapy is a valuable form of therapy for many people and it may be for you. Within the group there may be members who are able to put into words some of the thoughts or feelings that you have been unable to express. The gentle caring and understanding of the others in the group may encourage you to find new and better ways of expressing yourself and relating to others. The insights of these group members, who may be grappling with the same problem, may help you to understand how other people experience or relate to you. The sensitivity of the different members of the group and their concern for you may be just what you've been wanting.

Some groups are for couples only. Within such groups, husbands and wives may learn to understand each other better by listening to and observing other people as they express their fears, angers, hostilities, affection, love, and tenderness in new and different ways. In trying to express themselves to others, they may open up feelings about themselves and each other, feelings that may have been suppressed for years.

Some therapists prefer to work within the context of a group, believing that the interaction of the group members with each other and with the therapist enhances personal growth and facilitates therapy. Often, group therapy is used in conjunction with individual and/or marital therapy. Whatever the method of implementation, group therapy is a valuable approach to counseling and is certainly worth considering if the counselor suggests it for you.

WHICH KIND OF COUNSELING OR THERAPY IS BEST FOR YOU?

The kind of counseling or therapy you choose depends largely on the counselor you choose. That choice also depends on the nature of the problems you are facing and the recommendations of your friends, family, or any other referral source. Again, choosing the counseling techniques to be used is not as important as finding a counselor with whom you feel comfortable and with whom you work well. The counselor, with his professional training, uses the skills and techniques he considers most applicable.

Dr. Judd Marmor is one of the leading spokesmen for counseling and therapy. Speaking at the annual meeting of the American Orthopsychiatric Association in 1988, he noted that those counselors and therapists who get the best results, regardless of their profession, are those who are the most experienced, most understanding, and most empathic (most capable of sharing the feelings of their patients or clients). Regardless of the kind of counseling they practice, they have warmth, knowledge, emotional maturity, genuineness, and personal style, and they are able to relate to those who come to them for help.

Most studies have indicated that all forms of counseling and therapy are useful. Therapists and counselors regularly attend workshops, conferences, and continuing education programs to enhance and improve their abilities. That means that what they were doing a couple of years ago may be modified and improved this year because of their training and their professional growth. It is one of their personal goals to help you by working with the most valuable theories and techniques available to them. After getting to know your counselor, you should begin to trust him, but be ever alert to your own feelings and perceptions. If you feel uncomfortable, feel free to discuss this with the counselor.

If, after a period of time, you want to see a different counselor, you may make that choice. If you feel that you are ready to terminate, you decide. Talk it over with the counselor, but, most important, remember that **you are responsible for yourself.** If the counselor you chose does not seem to be the right one, or the kind of counseling he or she practices doesn't seem right for you or you just don't seem to be getting results, make a change. The process of making that change may be a good sign of progress in your ability to be responsible for yourself.

Making
the First
Appointment

R oger picks up the telephone and dials the number he has been carrying around in his wallet. The telephone rings twice and a receptionist answers.

"Dr. Thomas's office."

Roger hesitates a moment, then quickly hangs up the phone.

"What am I doing?" he thinks to himself. "Here I am, vice-president of a large engineering firm . . . in charge of a staff of professional experts . . . and I'm calling a counselor for help. I should be able to handle my own personal problems. . . . But what am I trembling about?"

Several weeks ago he called the attorney who had handled his divorce and asked for the name of a counselor he could go see. The attorney gave him the names of a couple of counselors with whom he had worked, and Roger had chosen one.

"This is ridiculous!" he says to himself. He realizes that he is rubbing his hands through his hair, the way he does when he is upset. He picks up the telephone again and dials the number. The receptionist has hardly answered when he blurts out "I want to make an appointment."

The young woman asks whether he's been in before and who referred him, and she offers him two choices of times for an appointment. He chooses one and the deed is done. He has an appointment and he feels relieved— this is the way he usually does things—directly and without hesitation. He considers himself a "take charge" sort of person. He likes to be in control.

When the time for the appointment comes, he arrives at the counselor's office five minutes early. This is the way he handles all appointments—always five minutes early. It gives him time to look around, survey the scene, and pick up clues about the other person. In that way he can be a little bit more in command. He learned this technique at the success seminar he organized for the employees of his firm.

With relief he finds that he is the only person in the reception area of Dr. Thomas's office. He had dreaded the prospect of sitting in a room with other people, waiting to see the "shrink." If others were there, they would be wondering what kind of problems he had. It was tough enough to go to a counselor. Being "on display" in front of other people would be almost unbearable. But it isn't that way, and he's thankful.

Dr. Thomas soon comes out to greet Roger and take him into his office. Roger likes his looks. His handshake is firm, a clue to Roger that he must play tennis or racquetball. He is dressed casually and seems to be comfortable with himself.

When Dr. Thomas asks, "Well, where shall we begin?" Roger feels the trembling begin again. "Well, you see, I've been going with this woman for about eighteen months. . . . She's a lovely person, and she has been very nice to me. . . . I like her a lot, but I don't want to marry her. . . . Not right now. . . . She wants to get married, but I just don't feel right about it. I guess the truth is, I just don't want to marry her at all!" The words just seem to tumble out.

Tears well up in his eyes. "My God," Roger thinks, "am I going to cry in front of this guy?"

Dr. Thomas sits quietly for a moment and then urges him to continue. Roger keeps on talking about himself. He talks about the most significant time of his life, when he was in college and working very hard on his education in industrial engineering while taking as many courses as possible in the business college. He knew that he wanted to be an engineer but he also wanted to be well prepared to move into the management end of the business. Working so hard meant that he had relatively little time for a social life. Marcia, his college girlfriend, understood and accepted the limitations he imposed upon himself and their relationship. He was goal driven. She believed in him and his goals and was committed to helping him achieve them while she was completing her degree in journalism. They agreed to postpone marriage until he finished his five-year degree program. She finished college one year ahead of him and secured a position as a reporter on a local newspaper. They lived together during his last year of college. When he got his first full-time job, they married, and a year later they had the first of their two children. Two years later their second child was born. All during that period Roger worked just as hard as he had in college. He drove himself, trying to climb the corporate ladder as rapidly as possible, and he was successful. In business, that is, he admits to Dr. Thomas.

He recalls that those had been difficult years for Marcia. She had been left with the children while he spent long hours and weeks at work, taking seminars and workshops, doing everything possible to secure the approval of his employers. She became more and more disenchanted with their marriage. He was praised for his ability as a communicator in business, but Marcia found that he communicated little to her and the children. She gave up on the marriage and asked him for a divorce. He was disappointed but agreed. After the divorce he found that he missed her and the children, but he threw himself into his work even more intensely. Much to his surprise, his love for the children seems to grow as he is farther away from them. They live with Marcia and see him on alternate weekends.

As the session goes on, Roger finds himself wondering about his behavior. He tells of meeting Terry, one of the new women in his company, and talks about how she reminds him of Marcia. She is tender, loving, thoughtful, bright . . . all of the things he liked about Marcia. He's established a relationship with her, but he's having some of the same difficulties he had with Marcia. He is always involved in work and employee relationships. He's traveling more than before and has to call off plans that he's made with Terry because of the demands of the travel. She seems to understand, but complains to him about her disappointments. That increases his feeling of tension and confusion. Is he on the wrong track? Is it impossible for him to have a meaningful relationship with a woman?

After about an hour, which has seemed like only a few minutes to Roger, Dr. Thomas interrupts to say that the time for the session is up and recommends they make several more appointments. It is evident to him, he says, that Roger has deep and tender feelings for this woman and for his two children who live with his ex-wife. He adds that it might take several more sessions for Roger to sort out his problems and to make some important decisions about his life. Roger agrees and sets up weekly appointments for the next month.

As he leaves the office, Roger turns to Dr. Thomas. "These sessions really go fast, don't they? I didn't expect that."

CALLING FOR THE FIRST APPOINTMENT

Your first contact with a counselor is usually a telephone call. It takes courage to make that call. Almost everyone feels nervous, hesitant, and sometimes even afraid before making the call. That's understandable, because going to a counselor about your very personal problems is not a simple, everyday occurrence. It is a new experience and you're not sure about the rules.

But remember that nothing can happen in establishing a relationship with a counselor until you make that first call. *You* are in control. And you are responsible for yourself.

An important thing to remember is that you need not worry about doing the right thing. The counselor is familiar with the process and the feelings of those who are making an appointment for the first time.

Counselors do not call and solicit your business directly. They do not buy ads in *TV Guide* or advertise in the newspapers. Why? Because of their ethical standards. They leave it to you to call when you feel that you need help. Then they respond with sensitivity and empathy.

When you make the call, usually a secretary or receptionist will answer the telephone. In some cases the counselor may answer for herself. Now is the time to tell the counselor or receptionist or secretary what it is that you are concerned about. There is no need to go into details. It's enough to say, "I have some concerns that are troubling me and I'd like some information about an appointment." If you have been referred, this is the time to mention who referred you. And, of course, you must identify yourself and agree upon the time to meet.

If you have questions that you wonder about, this is a good time to ask about them. You might want to ask things like:

> Do you (or, if you speak with the receptionist, does he) work with the problems I'm concerned about?
> What are the fees or the cost of an appointment?
> How soon may I have an appointment?
> How long are the appointments?
> If I would like to bring my husband (wife), child or children (or any other person), may I do so?

If you have a question that you are afraid to ask because you think it may sound silly, ask it. The only silly question is the one that you don't ask.

At the time of the first call, ask whatever is on your mind. If the answers are not what you want to hear, you have the freedom to choose to make no appointment at that time. You may say, "Thank you, I'll think about these things and call back later if I want an appointment." If the responses by the person receiving your call clearly answer your questions, then go ahead and make your first appointment.

Don't be put off by responses that do not seem to relieve all of your fears. Sometimes it is necessary to move ahead and make an appointment knowing that you may terminate after the first session if you are dissatisfied. Be brave, for you are embarking on a process that will help you to become more self-confident, self-sufficient, and competent. Counselors are there to help you accomplish that, and you are the judge regarding the value of what you are doing. You must never give up responsibility for yourself and your choices.

PLANNING FOR THE FIRST APPOINTMENT

As you think about your first appointment, begin with such simple things as planning how to get to the counselor's office. Where is it located? Do you know where to park? If you are riding public transportation, where is the bus stop? How long does it take to get there? The reason for calling attention to these relatively simple things is that you want to avoid wasting your time trying to find the office at the last minute. Many times people come to the first appointment breathless, upset, and apologetic for being late. They waste time trying to find the place and then waste more time explaining their reasons for being late, lost, or confused. It's much better to arrive a little before the appointment, with time to sit quietly in the waiting room reviewing what you want to talk about.

The brief period in the waiting room gives you a chance to look around the room and consider the magazines that the counselor provides, the kind of pictures on the wall, the kind of furniture and decor. All of these things give you a little bit of an insight into the kind of person you will be seeing.

Some people wonder if it is acceptable or appropriate to bring notes to the first session. By all means, bring whatever you feel will be helpful to you. A counseling session is for *you*. There is no contest. The counselor is your ally and wants you to be as comfortable as possible. He or she will not be "psychoanalyzing" you and every word you utter or every move you make.

PRIVACY IN THE COUNSELOR'S OFFICE

Some clients are uncomfortable about being in a waiting room with other people at the counselor's office. They do not want to run the risk of being seen by someone they know, or they are fearful of the speculation of others about them and what their problems might be. Counselors are very sensitive to this concern and set up their offices and waiting rooms to minimize contact between those who have appointments. Usually they separate clients/patients by space and by appointment times. Their waiting room is not like that of a pediatrician or obstetrician where there are many, many patients all waiting to have their five minutes with the doctor.

In large clinics and counseling centers, the possibility of meeting or seeing others is not easy to avoid. Where several counselors are practicing together, it is possible that several people will be in the waiting room at the same time. Just remember that each person in the counselor's office is there in order to make his or her life more meaningful—the same reason you're there.

Some clients are concerned that others may hear what they are talking about in the counselor's office. In order to eliminate this problem, counselors carefully set up their offices so that they are acoustically "dead." This is done with drapes, furniture, and sound-deadening materials that will prevent others outside the office from hearing what is said.

THE GENDER OF THE COUNSELOR

The question of the gender of the counselor arises for some individuals. How can a male counselor understand the problems of a woman or, likewise, how can a woman understand the problems of a man? In this time of women's struggle for equality, for liberation, will a male counselor be able to work with a woman who is having trouble in her relationship with her father, husband, son, or other significant males in her life?

On the other hand, will a male counselor be *more* helpful than a female to a woman in the struggle for a meaningful relationship with a man? Similarly, will a man find more help from a female counselor for his problems with women?

There are no definitive answers for these questions. Professionally trained counselors have had to deal with these issues as an important part of their training. They have had to learn to work with individuals, couples, and families through study and through supervision of their work. These issues have been faced and, in the main, resolved. You may rest assured that the counselors will do their professional best to avoid letting sexual differences or similarities interfere with the progress in counseling. The counselor has been trained to work with you, whatever your gender or your sexual preference.

If there is a problem, it may be within the attitudes and feelings of the client. If difficulties seem to arise, talk about them and feel free to request a change or to withdraw from the counseling relationship. More likely, the problem will be worked through.

The same holds true for racial and ethnic differences. Well-trained counselors are able to work with individuals, couples, and families from all kinds of backgrounds and racial and cultural groups. These are very important issues and may be talked about in the counseling process.

If you feel that you must have a counselor of the same sex or same racial or ethnic group, you increase the difficulty of finding a counselor. Your personal, marital, or family problems are more important than these differences, but you're free to seek a counselor who meets the qualifications that you determine.

SIZING UP THE COUNSELOR

When you are admitted into the inner office of the counselor, she will usually rise to greet you and offer you a place to sit. You're free to accept the offer or to sit where you like. Again, as in the waiting room, look around at the kind of furniture, the location of things, objects, decorations, pictures, hangings, and whatever is in the office. All of these things will help you arrive at a feeling about the person you are seeing.

What is the appearance of the counselor? How is she dressed? Are her clothes formal or casual, comfortable or stiff, businesslike or relaxed? Again, these things will give you some clues about the person.

Look for diplomas and other kinds of certificates that will indicate the universities from which she has secured degrees and will show membership in professional organizations and involvement in professional activities. These should be hanging on the wall in the office. Professional organizations usually require that membership certificates be displayed.

This is the appropriate time to ask about her educational background and training. Ask where she was educated, what kind of training she has had, what professional organizations she belongs to and any other questions that you may have about her life or background. If you are going in for marital or family-related problems, it is appropriate to ask about the counselor's marital and family status, whether married or divorced. Any children? Ask about religious affiliation, if this is important to you. Since you are exposing yourself, your lifestyle, and your innermost thoughts, it is alright to ask about these things. You should feel comfortable asking the things that you want to know about the counselor.

At the same time, the counselor will be looking you over, asking some questions in order to learn about you and who you are. That too is alright. You want your counselor to learn as much about you as possible and as quickly as possible. All this is necessary and valuable in working with her to accomplish your goals.

The questions the counselor will ask to learn about you —your name, age, marital status, children (if any), educational background, employment, and interests—will be basic. Sometimes the receptionist will secure this information from you before you see the counselor. The receptionist will give it to the counselor just before you enter the office.

After these preliminaries the counselor will usually ask what it is that you would like to talk about. What is going on in your life? What is troubling you? Now you can begin telling her what problems you're having. Don't worry about being exact or having everything in chronological order. It is most helpful to you and to the counselor if you can say something that gets right to the heart of the problem, as you see it.

"My wife wants a divorce and I don't. She's having an affair with my best friend."

"I have a serious drinking problem."

"I want to stop smoking."

"I'm obsessed with thoughts of suicide ever since I found out that I'm pregnant, and my boyfriend wants me to get an abortion."

"My mother died, and I can't seem to get over it."

"I just found out that my husband is having an affair, and I don't know what I should do about it. Maybe I should get a divorce, but I don't want to break up the family. I'm all mixed up."

"I'm afraid to go out of my house."

The list of problems brought to counselors is almost endless.

Again, there is no need to try to put the problems in a particular order or terminology. No one knows just how you feel as well as you do, and telling the counselor in the simplest terms is probably the best way to convey to her the nature of the problems that are troubling you and the depth of your feelings about them. If the counselor wants some additional information, she will ask for it. The same is true if the counselor wants more background or a specific chronology. You do not have to feel responsible for anticipating or filling in all the details. Just tell it as it comes to you.

SETTING UP THE CONTRACT FOR COUNSELING

As you terminate the first session it will be necessary for you to make a decision. How did you feel about this counselor? What kind of "vibes" did you feel? How comfortable were you with her manner, personality, and way of working with you? The session will end with a question about your next appointment. You may feel that you didn't get all the answers to your problem or problems. Counseling is not a process wherein you present the counselor with a problem or several problems and she gives you the answer or answers. It is, instead, a process in which you open yourself to another person so that you can deal with life more competently and comfortably. It's a process in which you come to know yourself better than ever before. That cannot be accomplished within one hour.

The counselor may recommend that you make a series of appointments for the next month or two. Since most problems are complex, several sessions are needed to reach an understanding of what is really involved. However, keep open the option of concluding the sessions after the first series if you wish. Beware of signing up for a long series of sessions. Keep the situation within your own control and financial ability, but remember that you have some serious problems that developed over time, and time will be required to work them out. Most counselors will be understanding and will help you to keep your options open.

The counselor will expect payment on a regular basis. This should be discussed at the time of the first appointment, not left for later discussion. If the counselor does not explain the charges and payment plan, you must ask for clarification. Be sure that you understand the arrangement of how you should pay. This will be discussed in more detail in the next chapter.

HOW LONG DO YOU STAY IN COUNSELING?

How long one should stay in counseling is a very difficult, if not impossible, question to answer. For some, counseling is a crisis intervention, helping an individual, couple, or family work through a critical period or situation. In such cases the counseling is short term—four to ten sessions. For others, the situation is more difficult and complex, taking three to six months of regular sessions. Counseling may take longer for individuals with addictions or those families with children or adolescents who are having problems in school or problems of delinquency, truancy, or addictions.

There are many other situations that may require longer periods of time in counseling. The nature of the problems, the ability of the individual to respond to counseling, resistance, frequency of appointments—all of these things and others have an impact on the length of time required.

And then there are those for whom a counseling relationship is like having a family doctor who works with the individual or family through the developmental stages which are basic to each person and family. This means a life-long professional relationship that is useful and growthful for different members of the family at different stages of life.

Making the first appointment is sometimes a difficult step, but the rewards of working with a good counselor are worth it. The first appointment is the time when you have an opportunity to explain those things that have been troubling you. More than that, it is the first step in taking responsibility for improving the ways in which you deal with life—a most important step indeed.

The
Financial
Arrangements

A s their first appointment draws to a close, Karen asks Dr. Martin about the costs for the counseling and the plan for payment. Dr. Martin replies that his plan is to have the client or clients pay the full fee at the time of the appointment. If the client has insurance, after several appointments or on a monthly basis, he will list the appointments and payments on a statement and mail it with the appropriate insurance forms to the insurance provider. The insurance company will then reimburse the patient for his expenditures according to the contract with the employer. Karen says that she will secure the forms from the person responsible for insurance in the personnel office of her company and bring them to Dr. Martin at the time of their next appointment.

The next week when she and David come in, she brings the forms but reports that the contract that her company has with the insurance provider will not cover marriage counseling. Karen is in tears as she asks, "Now what can we do? We thought that we had a good insurance policy. We counted on having some financial help for our counseling."

Dr. Martin replies thoughtfully, "What you need to do is to find out if your insurance contract will cover your counseling as an individual. If so, you can come in alone and David's participation could be in a supportive role from time to time. He could attend some of your sessions and participate as seems valuable as we work on the resolution of your feelings. Then, later, we may make some other arrangements for marriage counseling, as you desire."

Karen returns to her job and has another conference with the person in charge of the Employee Assistance

Program. This plan is acceptable, and Karen calls Dr. Martin to confirm her next appointment and tell him that she can continue working on the problems that led her to come in for counseling. She is the one who has been feeling miserable and has missed several days of work because of distress over her relationship with her husband. David consents to participate in the sessions according to the plan suggested by Dr. Martin. Karen makes several more appointments to come in alone now that she knows that she'll receive some financial reimbursement from her company's insurance program.

HOW MUCH DOES COUNSELING COST?

One of the first questions asked by those who need or want counseling is—"How much is this going to cost me?"

There is no clear or definite answer for this question. Costs vary from counselor to counselor and place to place. In addition, no one can know in advance how many sessions will be required or how long the counseling will take. The problems differ, the range of possibilities is wide, and people respond differently.

The charges made by a counselor in private practice may vary from $25 to $120 per appointment, depending on several factors, including the training and background of the counselor, the length of time he has been in practice, the "going rate" in the community, and the status and reputation of the counselor. However, the amount of the fee does not necessarily determine the quality of the service. That is determined by the education, training, skill, and personality of the counselor and how you feel about him.

Charges are also determined partly by the kind of counseling and the length of the session. For individual or couple counseling, the session is usually one hour. A "one hour" session may vary from forty-five to sixty minutes. The cost for marriage counseling or couple counseling is usually the same as individual counseling. Family therapy may cost more per session since there are often more people involved and the sessions are longer.

Charges for group counseling will be less. Most counselors charge for group counseling by the month rather than by the session and the charge is the same whether there are four or five meetings in the month. Group counseling may cost approximately $15 to $50 per session, and most sessions are ninety minutes in length.

If you choose to go to an agency, such as the Family Service Agency, the Pastoral Counseling Center, or the Community Mental Health Center, it's likely that the charges will be based on your ability to pay. The charges will be determined by your financial situation and will be based upon your income, expenses, particular or unusual family situations, etc. The charges will be calculated at the time of "intake," your first visit to the agency. They may vary from no charge to $80 per session, maybe more, depending upon the policies of the agency. Most such agencies are subsidized by the local United Way, the Council of Churches, foundations, or a local board of directors that raises funds for them. With such arrangements they are able to provide services at a cost that is usually less than the fee charged by a counselor in private practice.

In an agency setting you may have no choice of a counselor. Your counselor is assigned according to the agency system.

Since the charges vary considerably, you must ask for information about them when making your first appointment. Be sure to understand the cost and the arrangement for payment before you begin. Since you are the one paying, you should feel free to ask whatever you want to know.

PAYMENT PLANS

The simplest and most straightforward payment plan is "pay as you go." Every time you have an appointment, you pay the full fee. With this system you never fall behind in payments, you always know where you stand, and you don't overextend your ability to pay.

However, many, if not most, counselors are willing to extend credit and provide a monthly billing and payment plan. In this way you may write one check per month for your counseling. If you prefer this, ask the counselor about such an arrangement when you start.

Some counselors have adopted the credit system of billing via MasterCard or Visa. Payments are then referred to the credit card system used for so many other purchases. The counselor collects from the credit company and you are responsible for paying them. If you fall behind in payments, you are obligated to Master-Card or Visa and not to the counselor. One problem with this system is that the interest charges on past due accounts is much higher than on money borrowed from credit unions, banks, or savings and loan companies.

Whatever system you choose, be sure that it does not create a financial problem in addition to the existing emotional problems.

HEALTH INSURANCE PLANS

Counseling is covered by some health insurance programs, but they differ very much. Some will pay up to eighty percent of the charges under some conditions and for a defined number of appointments. Many will pay only fifty percent of the costs. Some others refuse to pay for any counseling or mental health services at all.

Sometimes the professional qualifications of the counselor may affect whether insurance policies will provide coverage for the counseling. Usually fully licensed psychiatrists and psychologists and certified social workers are covered, but counseling by others may not qualify for reimbursement. Ask the counselor whether she is qualified for insurance coverage.

Many policies will reimburse only for individual counseling and do not provide coverage for conjoint, couple, group, or family therapy. The reasons for this differentiation among the professions and the different kinds of therapy are not always clear but are decisions made by the insurance companies.

Payments by insurance are complicated and inconsistent. You must understand the situation from the point of view of the counselor and your insurance carrier before assuming your policy will cover the costs or a major part of them. Be sure that you know what is allowed and what is not by talking it over with your counselor and the company representative responsible for such decisions.

CANCELING, CHANGING AND
MISSING APPOINTMENTS

A very important part of your responsibility in a counseling relationship is to keep appointments as scheduled, to notify your counselor well in advance if you can't keep an appointment as scheduled, and to pay for an appointment if you fail to keep it.

When you schedule an appointment with a counselor, you have made a contract to be at the office at a specified time, the counselor has agreed to be there at that time to work with you, and you have agreed to pay a fee for her time.

When you find that you have a valid reason for not being able to keep the appointment as scheduled, you should call the counselor and request a change, and you should do so at least twenty-four hours in advance. Some counselors require forty- eight hours notice. If you fail to keep an appointment, you should expect to be charged for the session.

Counselors have policies regarding those infrequent situations in which they may have to change or cancel your appointment. The counselor should make the policy clear to you when you begin the counseling process. If it is not clear at the beginning, ask.

Counseling is not cheap. For example, fifteen appointments at $75 each amounts to an expenditure of $1,125. That could buy some nice furniture, a fur coat, or a stereo or help pay for a new car. But when you think of the misery of a bad relationship, the mental health of a child, or the dissolution of a family because of alcohol or drugs, the money spent for counseling is an excellent investment. Emotional problems are so powerful, family fights so destructive, court battles so costly, and divorces so divisive that the time, money, and work involved in counseling are well worth it. Cost is indeed a factor, but it should not keep you from getting the help that counseling has to offer.

7

How Does Counseling Work?

I know I need help," Wendell says. "My doctor put it to me straight. He told me that I'd better make some major changes in my life, or I won't live much longer."

Wendell has come in for his first counseling appointment upon referral from his physician. He is a difficult case with a record of failure. He was a dropout from Alcoholics Anonymous. He has spent four months in a hospital for alcoholism, and he is still drinking. His doctor's diagnosis scares him and he shows it.

Wendell has the shakes and his face is red and puffy. He lights one cigarette after another and has difficulty staying on one subject. He talks fast and jumps from topic to topic. But he's very bright and competent on the job when he's not hitting the bottle.

At the close of the first session, Dr. Parker suggests that Wendell's family be involved in the counseling. Anna, his wife, is eager to help and the children are willing to assist in any way they can. Dr. Parker sets up a schedule in which Wendell sometimes comes alone, sometimes with his wife, and sometimes with the whole family. They all join to work on Wendell's problems with alcohol, in addition to other problems that emerge during the sessions.

Not only is the family supportive, it is confrontational. There are discussions about Wendell's fabrications, manipulations, domination, and pomposity. He tends to dominate the sessions, talking incessantly without giving others a chance to speak or make their observations until the family calls his attention to what he is doing. Then he is contrite and apologetic. He wants to do the right things but can't help interrupting. The first

87

major accomplishment is that Wendell stops drinking and he and Anna stop smoking, supporting each other in the process.

While he is hospitalized, his wife finds much support and help from Al-Anon, the program for the spouses of members of Alcoholics Anonymous. Members of the group support her need to talk about the problems of being married to someone who is consumed with the difficulties of being addicted to alcohol. As is often the case for alcoholics with spouses in Al-Anon, Wendell resents Anna's involvement with the support group.

However, the counseling the family is getting helps ease the tensions and unpleasantness related to Anna's participation in Al-Anon. It takes many sessions and a lot of hard work, but gradually Wendell no longer accuses Anna of being so involved and dependent upon the members of her group. She finds the group helpful and supportive, but needs it less and less as time goes on.

Wendell's work patterns begin to improve. Eventually, under his leadership, the sales record of the branch of the company he works for becomes the highest in the country. He is rewarded handsomely and given national recognition. For this family, counseling has proven very successful. Nevertheless, when one of their daughters is planning her wedding, she expresses her fear to Dr. Parker that her father will start drinking again when their family and friends gather for the big event. This has been a pattern in the past. In order to deal with it openly, she and her mother join Wendell in a session in which they talk through their concerns. Wendell understands them. He participates in the wedding, gives the bride away, and is a fine host, entertaining and serving drinks to the guests without any problem. The wedding and the reception are beautiful.

Wendell and Anna continue to have appointments with Dr. Parker about every four months for the purpose of personal, marital, and family checkups. Several of the children make appointments with Dr. Parker to deal with their own developmental experiences relating to college, marriage, and employment. As a consequence of his own personal growth, Wendell established a program which provides financial support for employees in the company to secure counseling.

This case demonstrates how, as a result of a crisis for one person, a whole family has found the value of having an established relationship with a counselor.

A COUNSELOR, NOT A JUDGE

"What happens when you get into counseling?" is a question often raised by individuals or families who are considering counseling. One person, calling for information and answers to questions, asked, "Do you go in, one by one, tell your story to the counselor, and then have the next person go in and tell his or her story, and then the counselor weighs the information from each one, makes a decision, and tells who is right?" The answer from the counselor was, "That's not the way it is done—it's not that simple. First, a counselor is not a judge. The counselor does not try to decide who is right and who is wrong. Instead, he will encourage you to talk to each other so that each one will understand what the other or others are thinking and feeling; he will help you understand the problem or problems more clearly and to understand the different viewpoints and alternative solutions; and then he will encourage you to act on these new understandings. Simply stated, it's more a process of understanding than of trying to decide who is right or wrong."

Family counseling is a process involving interaction between the couple or family members. It is the counselor's role to encourage self-understanding in each person as well as an understanding of family members' relationships with each other and sometimes with outsiders.

When working with an individual, the counselor helps the person reach self-understanding and a better understanding of the problems with which the person is struggling. He helps the client to grow in the ability to find better solutions and more meaningful relationships.

To understand what goes on in counseling, it is useful to look at the individuals or families who come for counseling. One person may be a despondent man, deeply depressed. The next person may be a young woman there for a final session that will conclude a series of appointments in which she has made some decisions about her career, and who is now planning to move to a new job and a new city—progress in her life plan. Another appointment may include a mother and father with a sullen teenager who sits across the room, defiantly refusing to sit with his parents or to talk with them. He acts as though they don't exist. The mother pleads with the father to reach out to the hostile son, while the father holds himself aloof from the situation . . . clearly a family in conflict.

In the counselor's office one sees the whole range of human emotions—the human comedy, the human tragedy

—the human drama in all of its dimensions. *No* problem is too far-out, too strange, too difficult, too simple, or too "stupid" to discuss with a counselor. Any human problem is worthy of discussion in counseling.

WHAT HAPPENS IN COUNSELING?

The counseling process is work. It is work that *you* do—with the help of an understanding, empathic professional who listens carefully and well. It is a process that sometimes involves pain and requires courage. Often there are tears and harsh words. It is an effort—a major undertaking that you do together. The counselor doesn't give you advice or tell you what to do. That's not the role of the counselor and it's not part of the counseling process, despite what you may have seen in the movies or on television.

For example, what some movies and television programs present as counseling is a variation of psychoanalysis, a particular kind of therapy based on some special theories and techniques. The client or patient lies on a couch talking about whatever comes into his or her mind, with the therapist sitting in a chair behind the couch making notes. The therapist sagely interprets the meanings of behaviors, childhood experiences, and dreams, finding that the person's troubles began when his father gave his bicycle to his younger sister or when he, as a toddler, witnessed his mother and father having sexual relations, or some other dramatic event. It is unlikely that these kinds of episodes unduly limit or shape a person's views of himself or herself; or of love, marriage, or other important things; but nonetheless they are the stuff of which movies are made.

Counseling usually consists of the client sitting facing the counselor and talking about personal experiences, relationships, thoughts, and feelings. The client does most of the talking, while the counselor listens and encourages the client in the process of understanding, clarifying, and coming to terms with those events and feelings. Often, the counselor asks probing questions to help the client find alternative ways of dealing with problems. What do you mean by that? How did you feel at that moment? When do these outbursts usually occur? What are your reasons for making that choice? And so on. Most counseling is a process of growing in self-understanding, self-esteem, and self-acceptance, in which both the client and the counselor are active participants.

In some counseling, the counselor may help you develop a set of plans or a program of exercises that are directed toward diminishing undesirable behavior, such as giving up smoking, learning how to control anger and rage, or fear of flying or driving. Sometimes the client may have sexual problems such as impotence or the inability to achieve orgasm and want help with such problems. Many people suffer from feelings of depression, have suicidal feelings, or engage in behavior that will cause them to be fired from one job after another. People go to see counselors for reasons as varied as all of human behavior.

BEING AN ACTIVE PARTICIPANT IN THE COUNSELING PROCESS

Counseling differs from experiences with other professionals. When you go to your physician, she examines you, makes some diagnostic statements, prescribes medicine, and tells you when to take it and for how long. The physician seems to know the answers. She is the authority who tells you what to do and, usually, you get better.

When you go to a lawyer for legal advice you are asking for the lawyer's opinion about what you should do, and you usually follow that advice.

In school the teacher tells you what you should learn, makes assignments to reinforce your learning, and then tests you to find how well you have learned.

In religion the preacher, rabbi, or priest teaches by preaching a sermon or lecturing to a class, telling you the meanings of the sacred words, how it was, is, and ever shall be, while you listen, accept, and believe.

Counseling is different. As usually practiced, it requires active participation on your part. It is not a passive process of being told what to think, what to do, how to act, or how to feel. It is not having something done by an authority. In counseling you have an expert in human behavior, a professional whose role is to encourage you to examine yourself, your emotional and intellectual responses, your feelings, your relationships, your behavior, and your desires—in other words, to understand yourself. The counselor then helps you to consider alternative ways of thinking, behaving, or feeling and then to take some action to bring about change.

When they start out, many people go to a counselor to be told, to be instructed, or to be given answers, when this is the opposite of what usually happens. The primary purpose of counseling is to help you find your own answers for your unique and very important self.

You have within yourself most of the skills, the capacity, and the ability to handle most of the problems and situations that arise within your life. On your own you may have become stuck, overwhelmed, frustrated, or depressed. With a good counselor to help you, it is possible to mobilize your abilities and to make the changes necessary to move beyond the feeling of being distressed and powerless.

One client suggested that, to him, working with a counselor is like learning to ride a bicycle—the counselor lends a helping hand, provides some training wheels, and then removes that helping hand and the training wheels, but not before the client is able to ride the bike with good balance and confidence. The riding may be wobbly and scary at first, but then skill and confidence are developed, and the client rides off with less and less fear and then, after more experience, with exuberance.

In this explanation of counseling, the counselor does not ride the bike for you or spend a lot of time telling you how to do it. Instead, he or she helps you to discover and then try out the new skill. He helps you up if you fall, but encourages you to try again and again and again until confidence grows and you discover that you can do it yourself.

Who has the power? The counselor is there to help you find that power within yourself, to risk using it, and to discover how exhilarating it is. The process of discovering your own strength encourages you to use it, and being successful encourages you to learn more and to grow. A vital part of counseling and therapy is not only to work through or solve difficult personal problems but also to increase your levels of self-confidence and self esteem. In addition, as you grow in acceptance of your-self as a whole person, you are better able to deal with others, especially those significant persons close to you.

Counseling is not all easy. As in the case of Wendell, successful as his counseling was, there were moments of confrontation and pain for him and for his family. Within the process, there may be anger and tears as one examines mistakes of the past and works at reducing their effects in the present, to find better ways of living. In marriage counseling and family therapy, there may be confrontations, and there may be old hurts that need to be worked through. The process takes emotional energy and work, but the results are worth all the effort. With effective counseling comes self-understanding, which leads to self-forgiveness and then to the forgiveness of others. This is a valuable freedom, one which must be won back if it's taken from us.

In counseling, as in the rest of life, **you are responsible for yourself.**

Your father may have been an alcoholic or a saint, your mother angelic or abusive. You may have been born into a life of riches or one of poverty. These are things over which you had no control. But whatever the conditions of life you were given, *you* are responsible for how you respond to them. You have to work with the hand that life has dealt you. So find a counselor and work with that person to discover your own answers and solutions—and your own strengths and abilities.

8

What Can You Say to the Counselor?

*W*ell, I finally did it. I kicked Edgar out of the house and divorced him. It was so humiliating. Once I started the divorce process, there seemed to be nothing else for me to do. It all happened so fast. . . . I should have continued coming in for appointments. . . . If I had I probably wouldn't be divorced." Molly begins to cry and it takes several minutes before she can regain her voice and start to tell Dr. Johnson what has happen. This is the first time that she has been to see him in months.

She begins to piece together the events of the previous months. "Edgar had gone on the road with our new line of clothing. Late one evening I decided to call him at a hotel where I thought he'd be staying and a woman answered the phone. Well, I exploded. . . . I got him on the line and I screamed, "You cannot do this to me again! I have had all I can stand! And with that I slammed down the phone."

Molly continues. "I was furious . . . so I called Becky, my friend who had recently divorced. . . . According to all the girls in my bridge club, she got herself a really big settlement from that divorce. . . . And I told her what had just happened. Well, she told me not to put up with it anymore. She told me to talk to her lawyer. He'd fix Edgar for messing around again. . . . Well, she called her lawyer right then and there and set up an appointment for me early the next morning . . . and that's how it got started."

The attorney was very assertive. He told Molly just what to do. He prepared and filed a restraining order that would put Edgar out of the house. He froze all of their personal and business accounts so that Edgar would be financially immobilized and would have to come back to

99

town. Then he prepared the papers for a divorce. Molly says, "I was astonished at how quickly it all began to fall into place. I was frightened, but I guess that I just went along with the plan."

As Molly is explaining the situation and her sudden action, it becomes clear to Dr. Johnson that Molly has not even thought about the consequences of her actions. She had never discussed the idea of divorce during her counseling sessions. After forty years of marriage, she had seemed more interested in making some changes and keeping the marriage together. She would express sadness for her friends who were widowed or divorced. She wanted Edgar to change, to slow down, and to spend less time working. She even talked about some trips that she wanted them to take after he retired. Hawaii was one of her goals for them. She collected information about the grand hotels on the beaches. One time she called a travel agent to inquire about the costs of such a trip.

"Oh sure, Edgar had an eye for the women," Molly would say, "Through the years I had to get after him for fooling around with the young women who modeled the lines of clothing that we manufactured." Edgar said, again and again, that the women meant nothing to him, that he was just keeping all of the employees happy, and he kept telling her to keep off his back. They fought about his behavior, his drinking, and the way he handled the company finances.

Their family doctor had recommended that they both go in for counseling after Molly had consulted him about her feelings of depression. Edgar joined her for only one session but urged her to continue counseling by herself because she seemed so much better after confronting her unhappiness. He refused to go in for another session, telling her that he didn't want to listen to her berate him and put him down in front of another man. It was embarrassing to him.

In the early sessions it had been necessary for Dr. Johnson to lead Molly back to talking about her own feelings and what she could do about them, instead of only talking about Edgar and what he should be doing or not doing. Molly found the sessions to be valuable in helping her to regain her self-esteem.

After a while she stopped coming in. But now, instead of talking with Dr. Johnson about the prospect of filing for divorce and carefully considering the consequences, Molly had impulsively followed the advice of her friend and the attorney and as a result now faced the most difficult experience of her life without any preparation for it.

Their marriage ended in a series of courtroom battles with accusations and counter-accusations, each one viciously attacking the other. Much of the family money was spent on lawyers and private detectives. The business had to be sold in order for Molly to get her share of the assets. By the time the divorce was settled, they were both financially poorer and emotionally exhausted.

In the counseling that follows, Molly seems regretful. "If only I hadn't gone to the lawyer when I was so mad. . . . If only I had continued the counseling instead. . . . Why did I do it? Just to get even, I guess, to hurt him the way he hurt me. I knew he fooled around, but I loved him anyway. . . . Now he never gets to see the grandchildren. He misses them. . . . He wasn't all bad. Maybe he would have come in for counseling if I hadn't criticized him so much. We could have worked things out. . . . I hate living alone. . . . If only I had talked my feelings out with you, it wouldn't have come to this. . . . The lawyer says I won a great settlement, but who calls this so great? I'm lonely! I got the great big house, but it's empty without him."

THE MEANING OF OPEN COMMUNICATIONS WITH A COUNSELOR

Open communications with your counselor means that you say anything and everything that you think about during the counseling process. A successful counseling relationship is impossible without open communication in both directions—from you to the counselor and from the counselor to you. Any time you think you are having trouble understanding the counselor or being understood, talk about it.

In the time between counseling sessions, re-think some of the things you talked about in your last session. If you think that you didn't say something clearly, or that the counselor misunderstood, bring it up and clarify it at the next session.

If you dream about the counselor between sessions, talk about it.

If you wish that the counselor would do something, or not do something, talk about it.

If you remember something about your life or your past, and you're not sure whether you should bring it up, talk about it or ask the counselor about it.

If you hate someone you think you should love, talk about it.

If you have erotic or sexy feelings about someone you think you shouldn't, talk about it.

If you have a serious emotional crisis in your marriage, talk about it. If Molly had talked to Dr. Johnson about her experience with Edgar on the phone, there might have been a different outcome. She didn't really want a divorce. She wanted to live with Edgar but with some changes.

Everything that happens to you or that you think about is, or should be, something that's open for discussion in the counseling process.

At first, it may seem a little strange to discuss those thoughts and ideas that you've always believed you should censor or suppress. In counseling, you are encouraged to talk about the secret, hidden thoughts and ideas that you have, as well as those that you believe are more acceptable.

One woman said at the end of a session, "This is incredible! Here you are, a stranger, and I have been talking about my personal life, my sex life, my most intimate thoughts with you for almost an hour. And I've never even seen you before. I have never talked with my husband, my parents, or my closest friend so openly. I'm kind of scared." Her flood of words in the session, her astonishment at her openness, and her willingness to say that she was scared were all indications that she really wanted to get on with counseling. She was, in fact, one of those people who made excellent use of the counseling process.

In the same way, the counselor is free to talk with you about whatever he thinks is appropriate for your sessions. This is what is meant by "open communication": the flow of thoughts, ideas, and feelings going both ways.

Once you begin counseling, it is important to continue until you have worked through all of the things that have been troubling you. You should also discuss with your counselor any important decisions you are about to make together with all of the courses of action open to you and all of their consequences, before making any big changes in your life.

Part of the value of open communication and the freedom to express your secrets with the counselor is that you will come to a better understanding of yourself. When you put into words those previously censored thoughts, ideas, or feelings in order to understand them and yourself better, you are eliminating the "blame/shame/guilt game" you may have learned to play early in life. Bringing the censored thoughts into open discussion helps you to understand and reduce or eliminate them.

CONFIDENTIALITY

The whole matter of confidentiality is very delicate. There is much public misinformation about it, even among some counselors. They cannot guarantee absolute confidentiality, in all cases, about information revealed by clients, especially in courtroom trials.

Professionally trained counselors, physicians, ministers, rabbis, and priests each have a professional code of ethics that commits them to confidentiality. But only attorneys, with their "attorney-client privilege," can offer complete confidentiality before the law.

There are two additional limits to professional confidentiality. The first relates to professional supervision. Most counselors are required to spend at least two years working with a senior member of their profession who acts as a supervisor. The two meet regularly, and the senior person has the other one report and examine the way he or she is working with those who come for counseling. They discuss procedures, techniques, feelings, questions, and responses, and the kind of subjects that are discussed or not discussed. In this kind of close observation and supervision, the supervisor is bound by the same code of ethics regarding confidentiality. The supervisor need not know the name of the person or persons being counseled. Her concerns are about the way in which the counselor-in-training is working with the clients.

The second limit to confidentiality is in the colleague relationship some counselors have with another counselor with whom they consult. This differs from supervision in that the colleagues are equals. The purpose of the colleague relationship is to satisfy the counselor that he is doing his best work. It allows him to step back and examine what he is doing, with another professional who is objective and not involved with the case. This is somewhat like a second opinion in surgery. This kind of professional consultation has many benefits to the clients.

CONFIDENTIALITY AND THE LAW

Legal exceptions to confidentiality can be troublesome. Many states have passed laws requiring that counselors report to the local police incidents of reputed child abuse, sexual abuse, incest, spouse abuse, and other activities that may occur among family members, friends, and others. Some incidents may relate to the use, sale, or distribution of certain prohibited substances, mainly drugs.

These laws present a very real dilemma for counselors. No responsible member of society wants to see these kinds of behavior continue. On the other hand, reporting individuals who are accused of these illegal and/or harmful activities will violate confidentiality and may well reduce or limit the possibility of modification or improvement in the client's behavior through counseling—counseling that might be more effective than arrest and imprisonment.

All of this relates to society's own dilemma: does it want people who engage in harmful behavior to work toward getting better, or does it just want those people punished? Clearly, counselors prefer that people work through their problems and get better, while much of society prefers punishment to understanding and improvement.

In civil cases such as divorce or other legal actions, the records of all counselors, except lawyers, may be subpoenaed and the counselors required to testify in court or make a deposition. Most people, including many professionals themselves, think that physicians and clergy are exempt and do not have to testify. This is not true. In most states even a physician's medical records, or information given to a priest, rabbi, or minister must be produced in court when demanded. Only attorneys are protected from this requirement.

Since the vast majority of cases a counselor works with do not end up in the courts, these problems rarely arise. It is a good idea, however, for you, the client, to be informed about them. For your own clarification, you should discuss these issues with your counselor early in the counseling process.

GROUP THERAPY AND CONFIDENTIALITY

One of the fundamental rules of group therapy is that everything discussed in the group is confidential and may not be discussed outside the group. This is always clarified with group members when a group is formed and is discussed when a counselor suggests that a new client join a group. It is usually clarified again when a new member meets with a group for the first time.

Such confidentiality is necessary if the group is to be useful for each member. A major element in group counseling is the dynamic interaction among the group members. They must be free to talk openly about their feelings and behaviors. This freedom can exist only if the group commits to confidentiality.

If you are in group counseling and this issue has not been clarified at the beginning, ask the counselor and the group about it.

COUNSELING PROVIDED BY EMPLOYERS AND INSTITUTIONS

When a corporation, school or university, agency, or employer provides counseling as a benefit for employees or as part of a service to students, there must be a guarantee of confidentiality. In counseling, information may be revealed about fellow employees, supervisors, students, faculty, or others and that information must be kept confidential.

If you are in counseling provided by your employer or school, ask for clarification from the counselor before revealing information about yourself or other people. If you are not satisfied with the answers you get about confidentiality, ask for a referral to an independent, outside counselor who has no relationship to the organization providing your counseling sessions.

I have served as a counselor for individuals whose employers paid the costs or who provided the counseling through insurance programs. Never has there been difficulty—for instance, the employer asking for reports of the personal issues discussed by the employee. To the contrary, the only contact with the company providing the employee assistance benefits was confirmation of the dates of the appointments and the costs, followed by prompt payment.

Part of maintaining responsibility for yourself is deciding what to talk about in counseling. Be as open as possible in your communications in order to secure the greatest benefits in the shortest possible time from the counseling process. Whenever you have any concerns or questions about confidentiality or anything else, ask your counselor. Don't hold back.

9

The Stress of Counseling

*W*henever Betty calls, Dr. Daniels knows that he should make an appointment for her and Gregg, her husband, as soon as possible. She usually begins by saying that she has "a little problem" that they'd like to discuss. He knows her well. "A little problem" means that Gregg is angry at her again.

They have been in to see him for several series of appointments. Each time Betty has begun by understating the seriousness of the problems they are facing.

The first series began because of an unwanted pregnancy. She used the Pill because it was so reliable but neglected to keep an adequate supply. She ran out, didn't tell Gregg, and became pregnant. Their first two children were born only fourteen months apart, and they had agreed that they wanted no more. She was already having a difficult time with the two. Now, with this pregnancy, she was faced with the prospect of three children under four years of age.

The sessions that followed were very stressful for Betty because of her guilt and anger at herself for being careless and her feelings that she was a disorganized woman, mother, and homemaker. Gregg, a well-organized person, was of little help because he, too, was angry at her. He was busy building his auto repair business and had little time at home. Helping her with the children was difficult because of the long hours in the garage.

A second series of sessions began when Gregg discovered that Betty was overcharging on their credit cards. In order to keep their financial affairs under control, they had agreed to minimize the use of credit cards. Despite the fact that Betty had an adequate amount of

111

cash to manage the household, she had charged the maximum on both Visa and MasterCard. Gregg chose to get a loan from the bank to pay off the credit card balances in order to avoid paying high interest rates.

The counseling sessions became even more stressful when Betty revealed that, in addition to Visa and MasterCard, she had charged hundreds of dollars at Sears, Penney's, and Dillard's department stores. When the monthly statements arrived, she hid them. Because she knew that Gregg would be upset, Betty waited until the counseling session to tell him. As she expected, Gregg was furious. He swore, she cried, and their relationship became even more strained.

After several sessions, his anger and her guilt subsided. They made commitments to work closely on their finances. Also, Betty agreed to spend less time taking the children to shopping centers where she was tempted to buy more and more things. They agreed to stop charging. They even cut up their credit cards.

About six months later they were back to see Dr. Daniels when Betty convinced herself that it would be wise to have the credit cards replaced. Christmas was coming and she wanted to buy gifts. She called the stores and told them that she had lost her wallet with her credit cards and asked to have them replaced. All this was done without Gregg's knowledge. When he learned what she had done, another crisis erupted, followed by anger, guilt, apologies, and promises.

The current crisis began after Betty started to work, part-time, in Gregg's auto repair shop. She took the job when he needed someone to answer the phone, type, and do other jobs in the office. Betty wanted to get out of the house and away from the kids. One day she found that she could "borrow" money from the cash drawer when customers paid cash. She could put the cash in her purse, hide the receipt, and have no record of the transaction. She figured that this was not stealing since they owned the garage. When the accountant discovered the cash shortages, he informed Gregg. They hired a detective to find who in the organization was stealing cash. Gregg told Betty about this plan; fearing discovery, she called Dr. Daniels with a new "little problem."

As stressful as the previous series of counseling sessions have been, these are much more so. Gregg is furious when Betty explains what she's been doing. She couldn't admit any of it until she was with him in the safety of Dr. Daniels's office. "How could you steal from me? I have a good group of workers. I was so upset, believing that one of them was stealing! And here it was you, my wife! This is more that I can stand." Gregg storms around the room, waving his arms and shouting at her.

When Betty responds, tears are flowing down her face. "I never dreamed you'd be so upset. After all, we do own the garage, don't we? It's all our money, isn't it?"

Gregg explodes. He picks up his coat and shouts, on his way out, "I can't stand any more of this. I have to go." Then, to Dr. Daniels, "I'll call you and set up an appointment for myself. I have to cool off before I can make any decisions."

Betty remains, dissolved in tears. When she is able to regain her voice she asks, "How, oh how, can I get myself into these situations? Life used to be so simple. Now it's all so mixed up. What am I going to do?"

Dr. Daniels replies, "This is really big trouble. Betty, we have a lot of work to do if your marriage is to survive."

This case demonstrates how stressful some counseling sessions can be. Consciously, or unconsciously, Betty would hold back and then reveal information during the counseling that made those sessions exceedingly stressful for both of them.

STRESS IN COUNSELING

Strange as it may seem, such behavior is not unusual. Many individuals or couples hold back information or do not discuss a crisis until they are in the counselor's office. In the safety of this environment, when such information is revealed or discussed, stress levels will rise and there will be tears, angry responses, and arguments. But, in large measure, that is what counseling is all about—discussing, examining, and resolving those things that are too painful to talk about in other settings. Thus, counseling is often very stressful. However there is always a goal in mind. The stress will be reduced by talking about the causes and then finding alternative solutions.

Why did Betty continue to do things that would cause such trouble for herself and Gregg? Sometimes it seemed that she wanted chaos in their relationship. Was Gregg too harsh or domineering, or perhaps too involved in his work and too distant from his family? This couple needed more intensive and long-term counseling than they had been getting. Just working on the problems as they came up from time to time was not enough.

COUNSELING TAKES TIME

If we are to believe the advertising on television, on radio, and in magazines and newspapers, the goal of most people is to find instant relief from the many ailments of the human condition, whether the complaint is headaches, indigestion, nasal congestion, colds, allergies, or constipation. And the relief must be *fast, fast, fast.*

Unfortunately, in counseling, instant relief is just not available. There is no counseling technique, no therapeutic manipulation, and no medication that will give immediate relief from the agonies of anxiety, depression, interpersonal problems, or psychological dilemmas that are often a part of living.

How much time does counseling take? There is no clear answer to this question. It may take a few appointments or many. The amount of time required depends upon the person seeking help, the nature of the problem or problems, and the way the counselor works. Short-term counseling is possible for most people, while some others establish a long-term relationship with a counselor and continue to see him over a long period of time. But solving complex problems is never *fast, fast, fast.*

Prescriptions by the millions are written for patients who want something that will reduce anxiety, elevate the mood, or induce sleep, but none of these drugs does anything to solve the problems that led to the trouble in the first place. For many people, the drugs may make the problem worse or become an additional, and even more serious, problem, should the client become addicted to or dependent upon the drug that was prescribed to relieve the symptom.

Taking such medications, in times of personal crisis, is reasonable. It is only natural for people to want to avoid or reduce pain, whether it be physical or emotional. But taking drugs for an extended period is questionable unless those people who have such problems become actively involved in counseling or therapy to deal with causes. Using drugs but failing to enter a counseling or therapeutic relationship with a professional is like having a broken arm and asking for a painkiller, but refusing to have the broken arm set and put in a cast. The pain may subside but the arm is still broken.

Counseling is a way of reducing anxiety, depressed feelings, and confusing problems in a relationship. This is accomplished by facing and working on those factors that cause the problems, instead of trying to avoid or ignore them. Depression, anxiety, anger, hostility, dismay, fear, hurt feelings, sexual problems, personality conflicts, and many other kinds of difficulty are not, in themselves, the problem. They are only the symptoms that must be examined, understood, confronted, and resolved.

Many people go to a counselor for a "quick fix," an answer, a solution, a panacea, but it does not work that way. Some people go just to be heard, to present their case, or to justify what they have been doing. That is a beginning, but it is not enough.

The counseling process means bringing into awareness those things which, when left unexamined, only seem to grow bigger, more complex, and more difficult to solve. This means that the counseling process takes time and work. It means changing the way you think about and deal with those experiences and situations that lie at the root of your distress.

COUNSELING REQUIRES
SELF-EXAMINATION

Counseling is an active process of meeting with a professional counselor who helps you look at your whole self—your behavior and your ways of thinking, reacting, and living with yourself, your family, and other people who are important to you. In this process, the first step is to come to a new and better understanding of yourself and your ways of relating. The next step is to discover some alternative ways of living and being yourself, ways that will work better than those you have been using. To do this requires intense work, thinking, openness, and the consideration of alternatives, with your counselor acting as a catalyst, a guide, the one who encourages you to keep working.

SELF-EXAMINATION MAY BE
STRESSFUL

Because counseling involves looking at yourself, your ways of thinking and reacting, and your ways of relating to others, the process can be very stressful. Very little about you is left unexamined. You may or may not like what you see. You will probably want to make some changes.

As you look at your current problems, at your past, and at those events and people who influenced you, you may well find yourself in tears, upset, distressed, or angry. You may recall circumstances and situations that you had forgotten, experiences that were unresolved. All these things may be a part of the process. They may be very stressful. You may laugh and cry, your face may be red, your make-up smeared, and your nose runny. One man said to me, "I can't believe that I could cry again about those experiences. I guess I never did really work them out until now."

Counseling takes time and work and may be stressful but it leads to life changes. At its best, counseling can lead to self-respect, self-love, and the joy of learning much more about yourself and liking what you find.

COUNSELING LEADS TO TAKING RESPONSIBILITY FOR YOURSELF

The process of counseling may be unfamiliar and disturbing, even though your counselor is non-judgmental, a good listener, and understanding. While we are growing up we are taught the "blame/shame/guilt game." "Who broke that window?" "Who left the door open?" "Did you pick up your clothes?" "Who put the dent in the car?" "How late did you stay out last night?" Such questions directed at us seemed to be stated in ways calculated to create guilt and to make us feel bad for failing to do those things that someone else thought that we should do or for doing those things someone else thought were wrong. As a result we learn to be self-protective and to be careful about what we say or let others know about us.

In counseling you learn to reveal and examine what you thought, what you did, what you wanted to do, and what you meant. You learn to examine all those private thoughts and ideas with the counselor. He helps you not to blame, feel shame, or feel guilt, but to understand the thought, behavior, or idea, and to consider what lies behind all of those things.

In the process you discover that you can accept responsibility for yourself. You understand the reasons for behaving or thinking as you did, under those circumstances. You find that if you don't like what you did or thought, that you have within you the power to make changes—to act, to think, and to feel differently.

You learn that, no matter what someone else said or did, how you respond to those things is up to you. *You* are responsible for all of your responses. You no longer say, "He makes me mad (or sad, or happy)." Instead, you say to yourself, aloud or silently, "I choose to be mad (or sad, or happy) about what he said or did." You choose to be responsible for yourself and not to blame or give responsibility to others for your feelings and behavior.

In the case of Betty and Gregg, we saw that Betty needs to become aware of the real reasons for her behavior, the ways in which she does some things that create problems for herself and Gregg. And Gregg must learn that there are things that he does that help to set up the circumstances that propel them into their recurring problems. Counseling for them will continue to be stressful until they really get to work on the underlying difficulties and each takes responsibility for making changes.

The process of counseling—sharing your innermost thoughts, feelings, ideas, and behaviors with the counselor—may be difficult and stressful. The important thing to remember is that, with careful examination of yourself and your behavior with a competent counselor, you may change your self, your behavior, and your way of thinking and being—and find for yourself a better way of living.

10

Terminating
the Therapy
Process

*H*i ya, Doc."

Tom begins his telephone call in the same breezy fashion that he had when he came in for appointments on a regular basis.

"It's been about a year and a half since I was in to see you. Becky and I are still married and living together—if you can believe it. Young Tommy is still in high school and little ol' Suzy is having a great time with her pony. Since I saw you last, we moved out into the country and it was a good move for all of us. Now, I think it's time to come in to see you again. I still blow my stack now and then and that upsets everybody. Maybe I can improve if you'll work with me again." He talks in his rapid-fire way.

Dr. Thompson picks up his schedule and pencils in an appointment. "Sure, Tom, I can give you an appointment. I'd like to see you again. How about you and Becky coming in next Thursday, right after lunch. Say one o'clock?"

Tom accepts the appointment and says that he'll have to talk with Becky about the date and time.

As he hangs up the phone, Dr. Thompson thinks about Tom's response that he'll confirm the appointment after checking with Becky. In the past he would have taken the appointment and told Becky that she had better be there, whether the time was convenient or not. That's a sign that Tom is becoming more considerate.

Dr. Thompson reflects on his first sessions with Tom and Becky. They were referred by their attorney friend after

Becky called to ask for information about getting a divorce. Tom had become so difficult because of his drinking, gambling, and "helling around" that she wanted out of the marriage.

Becky started dating Tom while they were in college. He was the most exciting person she had ever met. She was very popular in her sorority, was one of its officers, and was a good student. Tom, on the other hand, was independent. He never wanted to be part of the fraternity group because he was always working on organizing deals that would earn money. He was very successful at doing so; he had his own car, wore nice clothes, and was well on his way to becoming a successful businessman even while in college. He became interested in electronics, learned how to keep up with new developments, and was always on the forefront with new business ideas. His energy, personality, and business sense led to the development of a highly successful company.

They married right out of college, and Becky worked with him until their son was born. She remained at home after that, and two years later they had a daughter. That fulfilled Becky's dream of a family. The major problem was that Tom continued to devote his attention to building his business. He was rarely at home, he traveled frequently, and, unlike during his college years, he became very active in business organizations and the social life that was a part of them. Most of the activities he engaged in kept him away from home even more. These activities were the source of Becky's discomfort with the kind of life they were living. Too much partying, drinking, gambling, and "running around" with a free-wheeling bunch of men led to arguments and contention between them. No matter what she tried, Becky could not get him interested in doing things with her and the family. Feeling hopeless about the deteriorating relationship, she decided to talk to their attorney. He suggested the counseling instead of divorce.

After about six months of counseling, they had reorganized their lives and established a much more pleasant and comfortable relationship. Tom gave up some of the activities that had kept him away from home. They bought a house out in the country where he could devote some of his time to developing his relationship with the children and Becky, instead of continuing the damaging behavior he had been engaging in. Then they concluded the series of sessions. But they agreed to return in about a year to review and confirm the progress they had made.

Tom's call was a good sign because, in the beginning, he had resisted the idea of counseling. He was converted to it after about the third session. When he found that Becky was willing to look at herself and not just blame him for everything, he changed his attitude and got to work on himself and the relationship. In addition to the conjoint counseling with Becky, he had a series of sessions alone, probing his own background and philosophy of life. He found the process to be very helpful.

Dr. Thompson considered this a successful case, one in which both partners made some important changes. The follow-up session should reaffirm the progress that had been made.

TERMINATING COUNSELING

As with many other important experiences, counseling does not end with a clear and easily definable conclusion.

There is no granting of a certificate or diploma, no graduation ceremony.

Counseling or therapy is a process, a series of developmental stages, which, as they are passed through, may result in an awareness, a feeling that the time has arrived for this meaningful relationship to change. The counselor may call attention to it, or you, the client/patient, may have the feeling that the time has come.

For some, there is a feeling of relief that your problems have been resolved and you don't have to come in for sessions anymore. For others, there may be a kind of sadness about concluding such a significant and important part of your life.

In some counseling relationships, there are contracts in which the end is determined at the beginning. In other words, the agreement between you and the counselor states that there will be a series of five, eight, or twenty sessions, or a specified number of appointments over three months, or that the sessions will conclude when the school term ends, or the divorce is granted, or at some other stated time.

In other counseling arrangements, the series of appointments may be open-ended—dependent upon the counselor, or you, talking about and deciding upon termination whenever one or the other suggests it. For one reason or another, you may want to stop the sessions before your goals have been reached—for financial reasons, because you think it is not working out, or because of suggestions from friends or family. At the other extreme, you may have developed a dependency relationship and be afraid to terminate. In any case, the termination must be discussed, clarified, and agreed upon by both parties to the counseling agreement, the counselor and you.

Counseling is, after all, a unique transaction. There are few, if any, other situations in which you may spend hour after hour talking, at length and in depth, about anything and everything you want. The counselor may provide some direction, introduce some issues, and ask some questions. But your concerns, problems, ideas, feelings, and questions are the central point of the sessions. Rarely is so much attention focused on you. But this is all purposeful, and when the purpose has been served, the time has come to end the counseling.

THE TERMINATION PROCESS

The process of terminating a series of counseling sessions usually begins with the counselor. When he or she thinks that a client has made significant progress and achieved a heightened sense of independence and responsibility, the counselor may say something like the following: "Well, perhaps we won't make another appointment at this time. What do you think?"

Your reply, assuming you have reached the same conclusion, may be something like, "I guess you're right. I seem to have worked through my crisis. I think I understand more about myself, the causes that led to those problems, and ways to keep from letting it happen again. Sometimes I'm a little unsure of myself, but I'm doing much better."

The counselor might continue, "I agree. Remember, you're free to call at any time and set up another appointment, if you want to."

THE CLIENT'S ROLE IN
TERMINATION

You, the client, do not have to wait for the counselor to suggest termination. Part of being responsible for yourself is trusting yourself to know when it is time for counseling to end. In earlier chapters, we discussed ending sessions when you think they are not effective or productive for you.

You have the same freedom, indeed the same responsibility to yourself, to stop when you think the time is right. If the counselor has not suggested termination, and you think it is time, you must suggest it. The counselor may be waiting for you to suggest termination as part of your developmental process. Of course, it might be that the counselor thinks that you're not ready to end the relationship at that time. Even so, the decision is yours.

COUNSELING AND FRIENDSHIP

As crises are worked through and difficult relations are worked out, it is possible that you may want to remain friends with the counselor or to know more about what he thinks about other issues, problems, or questions, including how he feels about love, friendship, sex, his marriage, children, current events, and religion. But remember that what the counselor thinks or believes usually has little to do with the progress you have made in solving personal problems, or whatever you came into counseling to accomplish. Your progress in counseling is the primary purpose for the meetings, and the counselor will almost always dismiss or avoid personal questions directed at him and hold to the main purpose of the relationship—the resolution of your problems.

A counselor must maintain a professional distance from the client in order to be as objective and impartial as possible. But the closeness that develops between the counselor and you is an important part of the counseling process. The two of you must talk about feelings, the good and the bad, about anger, about hostility, and about love—whatever feelings are generated. They must be understood and then related to the important growth process for which you have been meeting. They must be worked through. Then, the sessions may terminate.

TERMINATION NEED NOT BE FINAL

Terminating or ending may not be quite the right words to use here because, at a later date, there may be additional sessions for the purpose of reviewing, checking on progress, and confirming and enhancing your growth.

One client, when calling for an appointment, said to me, "It's about time for me to come in for a checkup." Another called and said, "I guess I ought to come in for a tuneup." Checking up, tuning up, and reviewing progress toward goals all may be a very important part of your long-range growth. Reviewing what you found, what you want, and who you are becoming is an integral part of the whole process. As a part of this review, you might want to re-read portions of this book from time to time. And you might want to review the checklist of key ideas about counseling at the end of this chapter. The purpose of counseling is to increase your well-being, your success, and your peace of mind, and these things are important enough to make some maintenance work worth the effort. Although counseling can be costly in terms of time, money, stress, and emotional energy, the benefits really do far outweigh the costs. After all, how can you put a price on happiness?

1. Counseling is usually a short-term process with a definite goal or a specific problem.

2. Counseling may involve an individual, a couple, a family or a group.

3. Counseling is best defined by a clear understanding between the two parties—you and the counselor—about the cost, number of sessions, scheduling, missed appointments, insurance, methods of payment, and other arrangements.

4. Counseling is sometimes stressful. Stress may increase during the process, but the goal is development and growth through and beyond problems that have been troublesome, to the end that one can handle any and all life situations and relationships with greater skill and ease.

5. Sometimes counseling may go on for a long time, but that is a decision to be made by the counselor and client/patient. Some kinds of counseling may require a commitment to long-term work while other counseling is crisis-centered and short-term.

6. Counseling may be enhanced by follow-up sessions after the initial series of sessions has been completed.

7. Counseling often results in strong feelings between client and counselor which, when handled well, enhance the lives of all concerned.

8. Counseling, at its best, usually results in personal growth and a sense of strength and vitality in facing the normal problems of living.

9. Counseling is working toward self-responsibility. Whatever progress is made, whatever is decided, whatever is chosen, all of it is directed toward one goal—becoming responsible for yourself.

10. Counselors work to put themselves out of work. Their goal is to help you to become responsible for yourself so that you no longer need their services. With the help of a competent, caring counselor, you can find the freedom to grow and to change and to become a happier, healthier person.

APPENDIX

NATIONAL ORGANIZATIONS FOR LOCAL REFERRALS

AMERICAN ASSOCIATION FOR MARRIAGE
AND FAMILY THERAPY
   1717 K Street NW, Suite 407, Washington, DC 20036
   Telephone: 202/429-1825

AMERICAN ASSOCIATION OF PASTORAL
COUNSELORS
   9508A Lee Highway, Fairfax, VA 22031
   Telephone: 703/385-6967

AMERICAN ASSOCIATION OF SEX EDUCATORS,
COUNSELORS AND THERAPISTS
   11 Dupont Circle NW, Suite 200, Washington, DC 20036
   Telephone: 202/462-1171

AMERICAN GROUP PSYCHOTHERAPY ASSOCIATION
   25 East 21st Street, New York, NY 10010
   Telephone: 212/477-2677

AMERICAN ORTHOPSYCHIATRIC ASSOCIATION
   19 West 44th Street, New York, NY 10036
   Telephone: 212/354-5770

AMERICAN PSYCHIATRIC ASSOCIATION
   1400 K Street NW, Washington, DC 20005
   Telephone: 202/682-6000

AMERICAN PSYCHOLOGICAL ASSOCIATION
   1200 Seventeenth Street NW, Washington, DC 20036
   Telephone: 202/955-7600

NATIONAL ASSOCIATION OF SOCIAL WORKERS
7981 Eastern Avenue, Silver Spring, MD 20910
Telephone: 301/565-0333

NATIONAL BOARD FOR CERTIFIED COUNSELORS,
AMERICAN ASSOCIATION FOR COUNSELING AND
DEVELOPMENT, and AMERICAN MENTAL HEALTH
COUNSELORS ASSOCIATION
5999 Stevenson Avenue, Alexandria, VA 22304
Telephone: 703/823-9800